G000075048

Underground Guide
to
Los Angeles

- 2nd Edition -

Pleasant Gehman
Editor

Manic D Press
San Francisco

*This book is dedicated with love (and robot hearts!)
to James Packard, who said,
"I don't have enough eyes for LA."*

Special thanks and extreme gratitude to: Eddie Gehman Kohan, Iris Berry, Shawna Kenney, Natasha and Kelly, Meghan "Cupcake" Gehman, Taj, Valarie Bermudez, Miriam Chavez, Ben Mahmoud and Moun of Tunis, Andrea Ferrante, Adriana and Pam, Larry Johnson, and, of course, Dirty. Also to Skylight Books who have always been so supportive; to all the writers who contributed their time and considerable talents to this project, and most especially to Jen Joseph and Manic D Press.

EVER-LOVIN' DISCLAIMER: Just as almost everything in life is negotiable, so too everything is conditional and SUBJECT TO CHANGE without a moment's notice. A listing in this book does not imply endorsement. All opinions are those of the individual authors, and not necessarily those of the publisher or editor. All information is allegedly accurate as this goes to print but, hey, deal with it, okay? If you find something here that just ain't so, please be kind enough to let us know.

Cover: Scott Idleman / BLINK   Illustrations: Pam Hobbs
                   Production Assistant: Sarah Trott

          Library of Congress Cataloging-in-Publication Data

The underground guide to Los Angeles / Pleasant Gehman, editor.— 2nd ed.
     p. cm.
Includes index.
  ISBN 0-916397-81-5 (trade pbk. original : alk. paper)
  1. Los Angeles (Calif.)—Guidebooks. I. Gehman, Pleasant.
F869.L83 U53 2002
917.94'940454—dc21

                         2002012768

– Contents –

FORWARD!

City of the Angels, Tinseltown, Hell-A, El Lay...whatever you want to call it, Los Angeles is a fabulous, glamorous, unique place - after all, there's gotta be a reason so many people are still here after all the earthquakes, fires, mudslides, floods, and riots, right? For years, I've entertained the fantasy of leaving, but never can bring myself to even consider acting upon it. Los Angeles - no matter what anyone says - is not a cultural waste-land. It's an amazing, invigorating place. In fact, native Angelenos and diehard transplants would probably die protecting the city's honor. People from other cities think we're all crazy. Personally, I think anyone who *doesn't* love Los Angeles is the crazy one…. but I digress.

Like the first edition, this is by no means a complete guide - hey, could there ever REALLY be one? But this outrageously opinionated opus is compiled writings - including a number of brand spankin' new chapters - from resident Angelenos. The motley crew who contributed are writers, artists, musicians, ultra-hip scenesters, and professional bon vivants who know the best places to eat, drink, buy dirt cheap vintage clothes, scout hard-to-find vinyl, get body parts inked or pierced, see (or show) great art, hear new bands, and meet foxy, like-minded folk - all on a shoestring budget! There's even a chapter telling you where NOT to go! Years of collective research went into the making of this guide. Some of the entries will be familiar, some are serendipitous secrets divulged for the first time.

Because of the city's sprawling nature, you may want to rent a car. LA's transportation system (MTA buses, subways, light rail) is extensive, but awfully time-consuming. You may be stranded at a stop for ages between transfers, or stuck in our famous gridlock traffic. Cabs are plentiful but expensive. As with any major city, crime is a problem. Please don't be fooled by lovely pastel houses with manicured lawns and tropical flowers - any neighborhood can be a "bad" neighborhood, so keep your guard. Pick up a freeway map, or, better yet, purchase an invaluable Thomas Guide (a complete and coded LA street map) at a bookstore. You should also grab a copy of the *LA Weekly* or *New Times* (free alternative newspapers) for current entertainment listings. Another free fishwrap, *The Recycler*, has classified ads for apartment rentals, used cars, musical equipment, pets, jobs, and what-have-you. They're all published every Thursday. Whenever possible, URLs are listed. Please note that LA's main area codes are 213 and 323 (greater Los Angeles), 310 (Westside), 818 (San Fernando Valley), 626 (San Gabriel Valley), and there may even be more by the time you read this.

Explore and enjoy!
Pleasant Gehman

P.S. Several places get mentioned in more than one chapter - sometimes with differences of opinion! If a place crops up often, it's probably worth investigating - decide for yourself if it stinks or is great.

WHEREVER I HANG MY HAT...

PLACES TO STAY

Los Angeles, unfortunately, is not full of inexpensive, clean, safe places to stay. It's usually better to call up pals or a friend of a friend and see if you can crash for a while. There are, however, a few options that won't break your bank or scare you to death. If you have internet access, discounted room rates are often available online.

BANANA BUNGALOW (2775 Cahuenga, north of Franklin Avenue, Hollywood, 323-851-1129) Hidden in the Hollywood Hills, they are accessible to both LA and the San Fernando Valley. Dorm rooms (mixed or female-only) are $22 a night, and private rooms for two ($57) in the adjoining **GERSHWIN HOTEL** feature a king-size bed, bath, and color/cable television. Free airport pick-up and free shuttles to Disneyland, the beach, and other destinations.

USA HOSTELS HOLLYWOOD (1624 Schraeder Blvd., Hollywood, 800-524-6783 or 323-462-3777, www.usahostels.com or email hollywood@usahostels.com) Finally, a hostel that's actually walking distance from things you'd want to see or do. This vintage Spanish-style lodging in the heart of Hollywood features free pick-up to and from the airport, bus and train stations, free parking, a beach shuttle, laundry, storage, DSL internet access, and a huge, fully equipped kitchen. They have free comedy shows once a week, pancake breakfasts, and linen service, too. They also have tours going to Mexico, Vegas, the Grand Canyon, and SoCal theme parks. Spartan dorm-style rooms are $14-$18, private rooms are $37-$47. FYI: this place books up fast, especially in the summer months, so plan accordingly.

BEST WESTERN HOLLYWOOD HILLS HOTEL (6141 Franklin Ave., Hollywood, 323-464-5181) Located in central Hollywood, about a block and a half off the Boulevard of Broken Dreams, and a hop, skip and jump away from the fun 'n' cool Franklin Strip, this hotel has large clean (though unremarkable) rooms with two double beds, air conditioning, TV, and phones starting at $89. There's also underground parking, a large pool, and a tragically hip coffeeshop downstairs that serves great food at reasonable prices. Eat there and you'll also have the dubious pleasure of seeing, like, Deborah Messing (sans make-up) picking at a tofu scramble or Quentin Tarantino jabbering on his cell-phone while scarfing a burrito.

HOTEL ROOSEVELT (7000 Hollywood Blvd., Hollywood, 323-466-7000) has rooms starting at $159 (for a double or single room) and is full of old Hollywood glamour — and reputedly haunted — especially the ninth floor. Rumor has it that Johnette Napolitano of Concrete Blonde was thrown out one night for playing with an Ouija board near the elevator.

CHATEAU MARMONT (8221 W. Sunset Blvd., West Hollywood, 323-656-1010) used to be THE place to stay for down-at-the-heels artists and rockers, but has now undergone a chi-chi facelift and gotten extremely expensive — $280 a night to start with! If you wanna go all movie star or you're on some record company's expense account, you can book the private bungalows for $690-$1,000 a night. Still, if you can swing it, you might see Drew Barrymore, Courtney Love or Leonardo DiCaprio at the gorgeous pool. It's probably better to just visit Bar Marmont and have a martini.

THE DOWNTOWN STANDARD HOTEL (550 South Flower at Sixth, Downtown LA, 213-892-8080) Reasonably priced (rooms go for $95-$325/night, double occupancy) and beautifully decorated, the Downtown Standard is THE hip new hotel. Situated smack in the middle of Downtown La, an area that's undergoing a lightning quick era of urban renewal and hipster migration, the Standard attracts everyone from jet-set Eurotrash and international fashionistas to movie biz denizens, parents of USC students, and just plain old tourists. A big attraction is the gorgeous bar near the well-heated rooftop pool. Surrounded by the neon of the neighboring highrises you'll feel like you're in a scene from *Bladerunner*. The drinks served poolside are stiff, but you may feel stiffed paying eleven bucks for a cocktail. However, the waterbed cabanas, and the fact that the staff pretends they don't notice that the very cute (and usually pretty tipsy) patrons are skinny-dipping is definitely worth it! The Downtown Standard's slightly older sister hotel is located in West Hollywood (8300 Sunset, at Sweetzer, 323-650-9090) right in the middle of the Sunset Strip, within walking distance of many clubs and restaurants, including House of

Blues, the Comedy Store, Bar Marmont, etc. Rooms here run a little higher, starting at $135, but the location is a little more central. Both places have their high and low points (service with a smile? Perhaps not, unless you've been on MTV in the very recent past) but will definitely be more of an experience than staying at, say, a Days Inn.

FARMER'S DAUGHTER MOTEL (115 S. Fairfax, LA, 323-937-3930, www.farmersdaughtermotel.com) in West Hollywood, located directly across the street from Farmers Market and the new Grove Mall, this place is clean and reasonable, at $73 (for two people) per night. This would also be a good place to put up the folks.

PLANET VENICE BEACH HOSTEL (1515 Pacific Ave., Venice, 310-452-3052, pv@catricia.com) is out at the beach, full of itinerant Euro trash, but extremely reasonable at $19 per person for dorm rooms, $57 for a private room.

THE SHANGRI-LA HOTEL (1301 Ocean Ave., Santa Monica, 310-394-2791, www.shangrila_hotel.com) is also by the beach, and is a classic Art Deco building. Most of the rooms are airy suites (some with ocean views, but you'll pay for that) and breakfast is included. It's a Rudolph Valentino kind of experience, with rooms ranging from $170-$235 per night.

Another option in LA for long or shortish-term housing would be to drop by the **SCREEN ACTOR'S GUILD** (5757 Wilshire Blvd., 213-954-1600). There's a bulletin board with tons of rooms to rent, and sublets for apartments, houses, and condos, because so many actors are coming and going all the time.

A MINIATURE ETERNITY: Where to Eat
Suzy Beal

"A three-hour dinner to me is a miniature eternity, no
matter how good the food is. One of the reasons is
that while I'm waiting for the food to come, I have
to sit there and talk to people."   —Frank Zappa

There are lots of excellent restaurants in LA - the famous,
the pricey, the pompous - all easy to find via word of mouth
advertising, and the latest TV tabloid scandal. Who needs 'em?
LA is also the home of fast food, drive-ins, carhops, and experimental cuisine. Its spiritual pulse has always been along
the lines of the slightly outré. The places noted here are mostly
about breakfast, burgers, diners, dives, and culturally diverse
foods (Mexican, Italian, Asian...). Most are centrally located,
cheap-to-reasonable, and convenient to cultural centers and

things to do. So have fun, and as they used to say at Millie's: Eat, pay, and get out.

LOCAL FAVORITES

CHILI JOHN'S (2018 W. Burbank Blvd., Burbank, 818-846-3611) A strangely bleak white '20s box of a place with a U-shaped counter, serving chili and pie. Period. Well, okay... chili alone, with beans or spaghetti, hot or not. That's it. Recipe for delirium: a 103-degree day plus a hangover plus lunch here...

ALEGRIA (3510 Sunset Blvd., 323-913-1422) One of those strip mall sleepers that serves really delicious gourmet Mexican food at strip mall prices. Soft taco combinations, swordfish, tender meats in subtle sauces, appealing vegetarian plates. Top-notch regional cooking, dinners $3.99 & up.

CIRO'S (705 N. Evergreen, East LA, 323-269-5104) A truly great Eastside diner with a swell jukebox, killer salsa, friendly vibes, and world-famous taquitos (a half-order is about $3 and comes with beans, rice and salad). Order a little more and get the terrific guacamole gratis.

MI & MI (various locations) Casual outdoor seating and lots of good fresh Middle Eastern dishes. The combo salad plates include falafel, hummus, tabbouleh, baba ghanouj, mushroom salad, pickles, olives and bread, about 30-50% cheaper than similar places.

MAKO (1820 N. Vermont Ave., Los Feliz) No sign, no phone, no clue you're here, but the line at the little place just under the Los Feliz Theatre marquee speaks loudly: casual Japanese cafe food (teriyaki, sushi, soup) and unheard-of prices, $2-5. Hits the spot.

TO LOS ANGELES

EMPRESS PAVILION (Bamboo Plaza, 988 N. Hill St., 323-617-9898) Really fun dim sum brunch in a large, fairly elegant room in Chinatown: passing carts dole out dumplings, chicken feet, etc. (You may search in vain for rice or vegetables—it's all meat, sauce, sugar'n'starch). Add a cocktail and enter a guaranteed 2-day stupor.

SENOR FISH (422 E. 1st St., at Alameda, 323-625-0566. Also in Eagle Rock, South Pasadena, Boyle Heights) The latest branch of everyone's favorite fish taco place is in, of all places, the old Atomic Cafe—the ghosts of punk rock and baloney chop suey barely disturb the aura of happiness around the plates of fish, shrimp and scallop tacos with cabbage, salsa and crema $1.35 & up.

LA LUZ DEL DIA (1 W. Olvera St., 323-628-7495) At the south end of Olvera St., La Luz serves up various Mexican combination plates for $5 or less. Great carnitas and handmade tortillas, home-cooked beans; charming tiled dining room and patio.

BURRITO KING (2109 W. Sunset Blvd, 323-413-9444) other locations throughout LA) In a world of burrito places, here is the archetype. Corner stand serving great big delicious burritos — some like the veg version with lots of beans, cheese, guac, etc; others swear by machaca or beef or pork versions. Cheap.

INSTITUTIONS

...And who'd want to dine in an institution? If you're from LA, you already eat in these places because they're great, or you know people there, or the drinks are cheap, or... you have to. If you're a visitor, well, knowing these places is practically a requirement.

THE UNDERGROUND GUIDE

EL COYOTE (7312 Beverly Blvd., 323-939-7766) Gaudy, tacky, and cheap Cal-Mex fare. Bright decor and, uh, brown food. People come here because it's cheap and the drinks knock you on your ass. (Order margaritas from scratch.) The green corn tamales are edible.

PHILLIPE'S (1001 N. Alameda St., 323-628-3781) Downtown's beloved French dip place with sawdust on the floor and famous ten-cent coffee. Fresh roast beef, pork or lamb sandwiches (in the $3 range) plus lots of sides, pie, pickled eggs and wooden phone booths.

PINK'S (709 N. La Brea Ave., 323-931-4223) Famous Chili Dogs. Another landmark everyone has seen on TV at some point; of course the dogs are good and range from mild to caustic, but there is a system: 1, 2 dogs = okay; 3 dogs (shoved down = instantaneous projectile vomiting. I don't know why, but it works like a charm. Amaze your friends!

TOMMY'S BURGERS (2575 Beverly Blvd., 323-389-9060) Anyone who claims to know LA is required to eat here, it's the granddaddy of all burger shacks. People line up far into the night to inhale these delicious grease bombs. A weirdly incandescent SRO parking lot scene is surrounded by acres of crime...

CLIFTON'S CAFETERIA (648 S. Broadway, Downtown LA 323-627-1673) LA's most famous and peculiar Depression-era cafeteria with a North Woods theme: waterfalls, fake moon over redwoods, plus a teensy castle (?) with a religious diorama inside. Serves your basic meat, casseroles, and breakfasts, $2-4. They have a nice historical website, www.cliftonscafeteria.com.

DAMON'S (317 N. Brand Blvd., Glendale, 818-507-1510) Meat, potatoes, and Mai Tais. This Polynesian steakhouse has been serving the above since 1937, with a suitably modest set of sides: decent shrimp cocktails and a famously odd dressing on the salad. Old-fashioned prices, too.

VERSAILLES (10319 Venice Blvd., 310-558-3168) More lines, despite the presence of a second Versailles on La Cienega. But folks sure go for that garlicky roast chicken and pork, black beans, rice, and plantains. Entrees start around $4. Seafood and paella, too.

CHEZ JAY (1657 Ocean Av., Santa Monica, 310-395-1741) Fancy beach dive; big steaks, lobsters, good drinks, Sinatra on the jukebox.

FORMOSA CAFE (7156 Santa Monica Blvd., 323-850-9050) This ancient railroad car bar'n'restaurant creaks on, literally haunted by the shades of Gable, Monroe, Bogart... Food is just as creepy. But what atmosphere! Especially after a couple of their killer martinis or mai tais!

BIG FOOD AND OTHER BARGAINS

LA ADELITA (5812 Santa Monica Blvd., Hollywood, 323-465-6526) A Mexican pastry shop/deli in the strip mall that conceals the venerable Hollywood Forever Memorial Park, La Adelita makes hearty stews and tortas: huge sandwiches chock full o'roasted pork, turkey or beef, garnished with beans, lettuce, onion and salsa. A total bargain at about $3. (Eat 'em next door among the monuments of Hollywood's storied dead.)

DINAH'S (6521 Sepulveda Blvd., Culver City, 310-645-0456. And other locations.) A landmark family coffeeshop. Famous for fried chicken, cheap specials, and laughably huge German pancakes (about a foot wide and crammed with apple stuff). Deviate from the specials at your fiscal peril. Fun place to gorge.

THE ORIGINAL PANTRY (877 S. Figueroa Ave., Downtown LA, 323-972-9279) Open 24 hours and handy for late night meals. Famous for an enormous steak or chop dinners, unfinishably large breakfasts and welcome crocks of fresh crudités at the table as well as ancient ex-con waiters. Reasonable, considering the pounds of food you get (though profits enrich owner/ex-Mayor Richard Riordan).

AUTHENTIC CAFE (7605 Beverly Blvd., 323-939-4626) Insanely busy Southwestern/Pacific/ " creative", low-cost cuisine in funky setting. People keep coming like zombies; it has everything people can tolerate in terms of flavor and price.

EL TEPEYEC (812 N. Evergreen Ave., East LA, 323-267-8668) Yet another LA institution, but also a bargain palace! Most customers are at least second-generation natives, locals, and city hall types. Cheery, busy with unpretentious Mexican food, including the famous Hollenbeck Burrito, literally large enough to feed four. If you can eat two, they'll give you another free. (If you eat three I think they pay for the ambulance.)

ALGEMAC'S (3673 San Fernando Rd., Glendale, 818-240-8626) 1930s coffeeshop serving comfort food and good breakfasts in the $2.50-$5 range. Located across from Forest Lawn Cemetery, which makes it convenient for celebrity crypt-hunting trips.

PORTO'S BAKERY (315 N. Brand Blvd., Glendale, 818-956-5996) A large, airy bakery/sandwich shop with excellent inexpensive Cuban and American pastries, Cuban sandwiches, salady things, and small hot items — croquettes, meat-and-mashed-potato balls, meat pies — for pocket change. Ever heard of any hot food for 35-70 cents? Now you have.

LA CABANITA (3447 N. Verdugo Rd., Glendale, 818-957-2711) Recently voted best taco in LA (if such a thing is even possible in the world capitol of Mexican food), this cozy place in the Glendale foothills is worth the drive. Several kinds of tacos that are all different and all amazing— when we tried them we literally laughed out loud with pleasure, and we weren't drunk!

BREAKFAST AND LIGHT MEALS
PANTRY BAKERY AND SANDWICH SHOP (875 S. Figueroa St., Downtown LA, 323-972-9279) Yep, it's that place directly north and attached to the regular Pantry. Why there are two, who knows? It's more breakfasty than the steaky Original Pantry next door, plus burgers, melts, flapjacks, and big portions. Reasonable.

RAE'S (2901 Pico Blvd., Santa Monica, 310-828-7937) The extremely stylish turquoise 1950s diner Americans have seen in countless videos and films. But it's real regular roadside food: cottage fries, biscuits, sandwiches and cheerfully low-key. As great as it looks, it's no Le Dome, but still one of the few genuine diners in LA...

DU-PAR'S (6333 W. 3rd St., at Fairfax, LA, 323-933-8446) Kind of run-of-the-mill '50s coffeeshop but rabid fans like their understandably famous breakfasts and pies — blueberry cream cheese, apple, pecan, strawberry... the only diner in the free-for-all food mall at the Farmers Market.

THE UNDERGROUND GUIDE

ROSCOE'S CHICKEN AND WAFFLES (1514 N. Gower St., Hollywood, 323-466-7453 and other locations) Talk about your heart attack on a plate! But what a delicious way to go: enormous pieces of fried chicken, mashed potatoes, grits, greens... and waffles drenched in butter and syrup.

MILLIE'S (3828 W. Sunset Blvd., Silverlake, 323-664-0404) Everyone eats here sooner or later. Vintage diner serving big breakfasts with garlicky rosemary cottage fries, strong coffee, biscuits and gravy plus a swell old jukebox. Super popular with Silverlake and Hollywood types. Thankfully, the newest owners don't think it's "cute" to berate and throw things at customers, as was the fashion here, so all can feel welcome.

UNCLE BILL'S PANCAKE HOUSE (1305 Highland Ave., Manhattan Beach, 310-545-8777) The long wait tells you the huge breakfasts, waffles with cheese and bacon, etc., are just what the doctor ordered. Especially when you add juicy burgers and big ol' dinners...

MUSSO AND FRANK'S GRILL (6667 Hollywood Blvd., Hollywood, 323-467-5123) "The Oldest Restaurant in Hollywood" (think Hammett, Fitzgerald, et al) can also have an attitude that gets old at times. Expensive, too, but two people can order a bacon and eggs breakfast, excellent coffee, and the famous Flannel Cakes, and share. The latter taste like big soft fortune cookies and are one of the menu's real bargains.

101 COFFEE SHOP (6145 Franklin Ave., Hollywood, 323-467-7678) Situated at a motor hotel, featured in the movie *Swingers*, it's got a noisy, retro/wacky style interior and a youngish crowd. Big portions.

JOHN O'GROAT'S (10516 W. Pico Blvd., 310-204-0692) The Lincoln Monument of breakfast places. Fresh biscuits, pork chops. People swear (albeit politely) by this place; now serving homestyle weekend dinners.

THE TOASTED BUN (808 E. California St., Glendale, 818-244-6416) Indifferent coffee shop, but it's edible in a dustbowl way, and it's fun to have someone meet you at The Toasted Bun.

BAKERIES

CELAYA BAKERY (1630 W. Sunset Blvd., LA, 213-250-2472) Mexican panaderia specializing in fabulous fresh bread rolls (this is where restaurants buy 'em). 20 cents each!

THE BACK DOOR BAKERY (1710 N. Silverlake Blvd., 323-662-7927) Where everyone in Silverlake goes for Apple Uglies, Lemon Sex, real Hostess Cupcakes, and dee-licious breakfasts.

OLD TOWN BAKERY (166 W. Colorado Blvd., Pasadena, 818-793-2993) Chocolate Chocolate Chocolate Cake. (It's 3-layer classic devil's food with bittersweet icing and ganache.)

THE COBBLER FACTORY (33 N. Catalina Ave., Pasadena, 626-449-2152) Old-timey handmade hot cobblers of pretty much any type fruit you can think of. Reasonable, too.

BROOKLYN BAGEL BAKERY (2217 W. Beverly Blvd., LA, 213-413- 4114) This is where lots of restaurants order their supposedly homemade bagels — go there yourself and get the freshest, warmest bagels in town.

FOOD TO GO!

MONTE CARLO'S PINNOCHIO RESTAURANT (3103 West Magnolia Blvd., Burbank, 818-845-3516) Regular homey sitdown place, but with large buffet counter chock fulla old-fashioned Italian food you can take out. More than you can finish, and reasonable.

BBQ KING (867 W. Sunset Blvd., LA, 213-972-1928) Beef ribs, hot links, spicy beans, tri-tip, chili cheese fries. Run by Texas folks. It's kind of a shack, but you can eat in if you really want to...

HAPPY HOUR!

McCORMICK AND SCHMICK'S (First Interstate Towers, 633 W. 5th St., 213-629-1929) Clubby upscale place at top of picturesque steps above the Central Library, but at Happy Hour they serve a bunch of $1.95 specials truly worth the trip: calamari, dim sum, oysters, mini cheeseburgers, etc. Plus, strong drinks.

BARRAGAN'S (1538 Sunset Blvd., Echo Park, 213-250-4256) Yes, good ol' Barragan's! Still the most comfortable and consistent family restaurant in the Echo Park/Silverlake area. Don't forget they got yer $2-3 beers and margaritas, plus complimentary nachos.

HIP HANGOUTS & AFTER HOURS

DAMIANO'S MR. PIZZA (412 N. Fairfax Ave., LA, 323-658-8761) Dark, teensy, New Yorkish, deep booths to hide in, open late: Damiano's is a port in a storm for locals. Lots of imported beers, pasta dinners, and reasonable prices.

CANTER'S (419 N. Fairfax Ave., LA, 323-651-2030) An LA

institution, serving semi-pricey (but authentic) deli fare. What draws the kids is the adjacent lounge with live music and the long hours where dates can wind down with coffee and terrific pastries.

SWINGER'S (8020 Beverly Blvd., LA, 213-653-5858) Swinger's has gone from being excruciatingly hip to institution status, sort of. Corn pancakes in jalapeno syrup; tofu scramble; American food – these'll help distract you from your too hip dining mates.

TORUNG (5657 Hollywood Blvd., Hollywood, 213-464-9074) Everyone knows this isn't the greatest Thai place in town, but we sometimes need a bowl of Tom Ka Kai at 3 a.m., and Torung has been meeting this need for years. Comfy booths, fish tanks, television and an endless menu with most items $4-6. Dicey neighborhood, and street towing after 1 a.m.

DUKE'S COFFEE SHOP (8909 Sunset Blvd., Hollywood, 310-652-3100) No longer located in the landmark Tropicana Motel (which was razed years ago), Duke's nonetheless oozes history from its previous incarnations as Sneeky Pete's and the London Fog (The Doors played here, of course.) Folks share communal tables or a counter and eat really satisfying breakfasts, especially yummy pancakes with added fruit and goop. Average prices.

JOSEPH'S CAFE (1775 N. Ivar St., Hollywood, 323-462-8697) Breakfast is kind of underwhelming, but the Greek items are quite good: tarama, feta and spinach snacks, Greek salads. It's also cool, relaxing, neat as a pin, and low-key. At night it transforms into, of all things, a popular nightclub with DJs and dancing. The best of both worlds.

THE UNDERGROUND GUIDE

PATRICK'S ROADHOUSE (106 Entrada Dr., Santa Monica, 310-459-4544) Beach dive for dining and stargazing. Burgers and breakfast. If movie stars make you sick, don't go there. Food's good, though.

THE SHACK (185 Culver Blvd., Playa del Rey, 310-823-6222) Well-named beach place serving burgers, beer, chili, and the Shack Burger: 1/4 lb. patty with Louisiana sausage. Full bar.

JAY'S JAYBURGER (4481 Santa Monica Blvd., LA, 323-666-5204) Big. Gooey. Messy. Yummy. Chili. Probably in top 3 rated burger stands in LA.

CASA BIANCA (1650 Colorado Blvd., Eagle Rock, 323-256-9617) Generations of locals love the old-timey taste and ambiance, but it's about more than nostalgia here — the pizzas are really excellent.

MAURICE'S SNACK 'N' CHAT (5549 W. Pico Blvd., LA, 323-931-3877) Fried chicken, short ribs, smothered pork chops, pan-fried fish; it all tastes home-cooked, which must be why people are drawn here like hungry kids. It can't be the prices, best described as moderate.

AUNT KIZZY'S BACK PORCH (4325 Glencoe Ave., Marina Del Rey, 310-578-1005) More well-regarded soul food on the West Side.

SUEHIRO CAFE (337 E. 1st St., Downtown LA, 213-626-9132) Spotless yet casual Japanese cafe near the Temporary Contemporary Museum of Art. Noodle bowls to teriyaki to huge trays of sushi, cutlets, dumplings, salads, tempura, and fried fish. Quite reasonable.

LA SERENATA DE GARIBALDI (1842 E. 1st St., Boyle Hts., 323-265-2887, also two locations in West LA) A universe of fresh fish dishes with incredible sauces of amazing variety and hue. Even broke locals go here for a special occasion. It's not the cheapest place in the world, but it is astoundingly delicious.

LA PARILLA (2126 E. Cesar Chavez Blvd., Boyle Hts., 213-262-3434) Bring a group and dive into a feast of table-grilled meats, guacamole, tortillas and sides. Affordable.

THE LUSH LIFE
M.X. Lingua

I was in New York, visiting The Library—no, not the stone-lioned New York Public Library—the *bar* called The Library, so named because it's full of books and leather armchairs and quiet conversation. The Library has standards and a doorman: you have to rate. At the bar, a gentleman in a gray pinstriped suit stood next to me. I ordered a sloe gin fizz, and my neighbor pricked up his ears, peered over his half-glasses. *Where are you from?* he said, *your accent.* I said, *Sodom.* The gentleman replied, *I knew it!* He gave me the once-over and leaned in. *Ever been to The Blacklite?* I nodded. The gentleman signaled the bartender to add my highball to his tab. *Do tell,* he said.

You're an astute reader and you haven't had even one cocktail—leafing as you are through this book to find a bar—and already you've noticed several things: this is a guide to *Los Angeles* and the writer inserted "New York" in the very first sentence. It's a little anecdote to show you that LA bars are known, even famed, across these United States, the dive bars as well as those behind the velvet ropes. I've had similar "Ever been to—?" experiences in Portland, Richmond, Atlanta, Orlando, Austin, Missoula, Flagstaff... the list goes on. And you've also noticed, since you are *still* craving that cocktail and are sober as a church pew, that when I called our city "Sodom," the gentleman knew exactly to which major metropolitan area I referred. With over 1,000 bars in the area, what are the criteria for narrowing the picks in this chapter? Consistency of experience. Locals frequent these bars not just because they're cool but because they're reliably cool.

TIKI BARS

It just *seems* like Sodom should be a tropical paradise. It's not, but step inside the **Tiki Lounge** (7910 W. 3rd St., LA, 323-651-1213, 6 pm-1 am, appetizers, Wednesday is traditionally a gay night) in Fairfax Village and after one flaming rum drink, you won't care. You may wander through several rooms lit by candles, and dawdle by the fountain; the place smells pleasantly of coconut, used in many of their delicious concoctions. **Tiki Ti** (4427 W. Sunset Blvd., LA, 323-669-9381, Wed-Sat 6 pm-2 am) is a palm-fronded shack on Sunset Boulevard in Silverlake, about the size of a nice living room, filled with tiki kitsch. Ray Sr., the original owner, was a bartender at the famous Don the Beachcomber's back in the '40s — his son and grandson keep the Tiki Ti alive, as well as calling out "Toro!" when tequila is poured, to which the crowd responds "Olé!" You'll see an interesting blend of local hipsters and old-timers, as well as tourists. **Trader Vic's** (9876 Wilshire Blvd. in the Beverly Hilton Hotel at Santa Monica Blvd., 310-276-

6345) also gets a lot of tourists, located as it is in the Beverly Hilton in Beverly Hills, but the feel of being inside a yacht, the fishing nets on the ceiling, as well as the souvenir glasses in which some drinks are served tend to also draw courting couples from the Westside. Trader Vic's has the undisputed claim of being the inventor of the Mai Tai—but after just one of these, or a Dr. Funk, or a Suffering Bastard; you're likely to believe anything....

MEXICAN JOINTS

If you're in a festive mood, you might opt for **El Coyote** (7312 Beverly Blvd, LA, 323-939-2255, Sun-Thu, 11 am-10 pm; Fri-Sat, 11 am-11 pm), a Los Angeles institution, having recently celebrated its 70th birthday. Crowded with trendy couples, groups of singles, business meetings and families, it's a convivial place filled with paper flowers, velvet paintings, fairy lights, piñatas, and sombreros. The crowd always parts for traditionally dressed waitresses in hoop skirts. Silverlake's **El Chavo** (4441 W. Sunset Blvd., LA, 323-666-5136, cash only) has a similar décor, but your Daiquiri might seem psychedelic because of the black lights. **El Compadre**, on Sunset in Hollywood, serves food until 2 a.m., and is popular with the rock'n'roll crowd for after-show dinner and drinks. **Lucy's El Adobe** (5536 Melrose, bet. Gower & Plymouth, Hollywood, 323-462-9421) across the street from Paramount Pictures on Melrose, is a favorite with industry types from both sides of the camera. It has a mellower vibe than the previous three, though weekend nights can be rollicking.

SEE AND BE SEEN

While all of these are authentic Mexican restaurants and bars, **El Carmen** (8138 W. 3rd St., LA, 323-852-1552, M-F 5 pm-2 am; Sat-Sun 7 pm-2 am) is the epitome of real Hollywood. The soft lighting almost obscures paintings which look like pulp magazine covers, and scary Mexican wrestling masks. This tequila bar in Fairfax Village serves delicious appetizers—order the potato tacos or taquitos early, because they're always the first to go—and often has a DJ. It's the crowd that makes this place "real Hollywood"—sophisticated late 20-somethings to 40-somethings in the arts or the Industry who somehow manage to convey intelligence not pretension, even when shouting to be heard. It can be a sophisticated singles spot, as can **Jones** (7205 Santa Monica Blvd., West Hollywood, 323-850-1727, Mon-Fri, 12 pm-2 am; Sat-Sun, 7 pm-2 am) near Warner Hollywood. Open less than five years, Jones Restaurant and Café (try the penne in mushroom cream sauce—yum) immediately became an enduring place to see and be seen. The dim lighting is not a deterrent but an allure— as are the rows and rows of Jack Daniels bottles decorating the joint and the nearly nude photos of patrons flashing their assets in the bathrooms! Another relative newcomer is **The Bar at The Standard** (8300 Sunset Blvd, West Hollywood, 323-650-9090) on the Sunset Strip. One of the first things you'll notice is the captive hottie (male or female) in the fish tank behind the concierge desk. The major drinking and mingling happens around the pool, whose deck is covered in aqua Astroturf, overlooking a terrific view of Los Angeles; the clientele are—or are doing a good imitation of—carefree young things who've made it in music or movies and have cash to burn—with cocktail prices starting at $8, they *need* to be. Down the street a bit, in the Mondrian Hotel is **Skybar** (8440 Sunset Blvd., West Hollywood, 323-848-6025, 11 am-2 am), now famous for the extra-large mattresses strewn about for lounging. The Skybar clientele is similar to The Standard, though Skybar's prices are even higher; and there tends to be a lot of pampered older men whose net worth may be extrapolated from adding up the price of their shoes, clothing, watches, jewelry, car keys, and plastic surgery. **Musso & Frank** (6667 Hollywood Blvd., Hollywood, 323-467-5123, Tue-Sat, 11 am-10:45 pm) is a Hollywood legend. The dark oak bar is in the larger dining room, and the barkeeps, typically older gentlemen from the era when good service was a hallmark of civilization, are generous with their shots. The famed martinis are poured from the shaker in a wee carafe that is served along with your chilled glass. Musso & Frank is known for steaks, celebrity clientele from the Golden Age of Hollywood, and for the fact that Raymond Chandler wrote most of *The Big Sleep* in a back booth.

When you want to dine and drink but aren't interested in the "Hollywood" experience, try **Ghengis Cohen** (740 N. Fairfax, LA, 323-653-0640) in Fairfax Village. They serve Chinese food with a nod toward the neighborhood ethos of Conservative Judaism. Ghengis Cohen is a haven for and champion of the singer/songwriter, several of whom perform nightly adjacent to the bar (separate cover). West Hollywood's **North** (8029 Sunset Blvd., 323-654-1313, Mon-Sat, 6 pm-2 am; Sun 8 pm-2 am) is unmarked. After 9 the DJ appears, spinning a variety of modern and alternative rock, though the selection varies according to the day of the week. **Bleu on Bleu** (940 W. Washington Blvd., LA, 213-745-4965) in Beverly Hills is nestled around the pool at Avalon Hotel. The bar scene in the alcoves around the pool is populated by young professionals from Hollywood and the Westside who want an upscale atmo and sophisticated cocktails. Out in Santa Monica, **One Pico** (1 Pico Blvd., Santa Monica, 310-587-1717) located on the beach in Shutters Hotel, has a long bar that's crowded on weekends; the quieter lobby with its beach-house furniture is a cozy place to meet a date or friends.

FOOD AND DRINKS

Do you need to lay a base for your night of bar hopping? West Hollywood's **Barney's Beanery** (8447 Santa Monica Blvd., 323-654-2287, Mon-Fri, 11 am-2 am; Sat-Sun, 10 am-2 am) serves all sorts of burgers and an impressive array of beer. Yes, it was Jim Morrison's hang back in the day, and yes, that's Val Kilmer as Jim Morrison in the real Barney's in the film. The **Snakepit** (7529 Melrose Ave., West Hollywood, 323-852-9390, 11:30 am-1:30 am) sits in the middle of one of LA's trendiest shopping districts, but tourists haven't found this place: a bar where bikers, punks, surfers, and neighborhood locals pop in for a bite—especially good nachos and salads. **The Kibitz Room** (419 N. Fairfax Ave., LA, 323-651-2030. Bar until 2 am; restaurant open 24 hours) plays host to the local seniors, as well as the flavor-of-the-month young rebels at **Canter's Deli**. The nice-grandma waitresses in pink uniforms are lately retiring and being replaced by t-shirted servers; still, the place retains its status as a haven. **Boardner's** (1652 N. Cherokee Ave., Hollywood, 323-462-9621) used to have a telephone at each booth back in the days of starlets; you'd call over to another table to flirt or arrange a date. Nowadays it looks like a pizza parlor with Tiffany-style lights, but they serve a good burger and sandwich, and the friendly bartender will often turn down the music and take a patron poll about which CD to play next. Down on Wilshire, the **HMS Bounty** (3357 Wilshire Blvd., LA, 213-385-7275, 11 am-2 am) offers a respectable coffeeshop menu along with stiff highballs in a wood-paneled bar that has portholes, other nautical accoutrements, sweet waitresses, and good prices: a party of four can munch on a couple of sides and cocktails, for about $50. **Cat & Fiddle** (6530 W. Sunset Blvd., Hollywood, 323-468-3800, 11:30 am-2 am) is a typical British pub and beer garden, and serves pub food like bangers and mash. It's popular with Brit-rock types, and one

Sunday a month a writer's salon is held here. Yes, really. On Sundays, Cat & Fiddle offers free jazz in its courtyard garden, a nice way to wind down the weekend. Since 1972, the **Rainbow Bar & Grill** (9015 Sunset Blvd., West Hollywood, 310-278-4232, M-F 11 am-2 am; Sat-Sun 5 pm-2 am) has always been devoted to rock'n'roll, in its location next to the Roxy and up the street from the Whisky-A-Go-Go. Nowadays it's a shrine to metal gods: the walls are covered in photos, autographs, gold records and it's still the hang of Lemmy from Motorhead. Two bars are downstairs and one's up, as well as an outdoor patio; while there's a small cover, just remember that you could be sitting in the same booth as Mick or David or Joan or Lita….

DIVE BARS

Has life got you down? Does work suck? Is your car on the fritz? Is your boyfriend being distant, your girlfriend being a bitch? It's time to go to a dive bar! Remember: "cash only" appears in the dictionary definition of "dive bar." **Hank 'N' Frank** (518 S. Western Ave., 213-383-2087, 2 pm-2 am) in Koreatown features original signage from the '50s with a shotgun layout, pool table in back, and mismatched stools along the bar. Call drinks are $3. Barflies and art students to Korean couples and Los Feliz/Silverlake emo-core types enjoy Charles Bukowski's once favorite local bar. Up Western Avenue is **The Blacklite** (1159 N. Western Ave., 323-469-0211, 6 am-2 am) drawing blue-collar workers, neighborhood Hispanic men, indie-rockers looking for an unusual experience and, around 11 p.m., prostitutes. But look closely, kids: the pretty Latinas are really muchachos under those tight little miniskirts. Black plastic garbage bags cover the catwalk over the bar, dating from back in the day when the rooms upstairs were available by the hour. The cleanest, well-lighted dive you're ever likely to visit is **The White Horse** (1532 Western Ave., 323-462-8088. 4 pm -2 am) even further up Western. It's a dive strictly because of its geographic location, though the comfortable chairs and couches inside are well-worn. It's a great midpoint to meet when one of you lives in Echo Park and the other lives in West Hollywood. **The Silverlake Lounge** (2906 W. Sunset Blvd., 323-663-9636) looks pretty crummy from the outside, but inside are pods of hipsters, locals, and gay caballeros. On some nights, newish bands play, and you can catch some great acts (check the *LA Weekly* listings). Weekend nights offers Hispanic tranny hookers, as well as a raucous bar scene with an entirely mixed crowd. The **Power House** (1714 N. Highland Ave., Hollywood, 323-463-9438. 10 pm-2 am) is still standing its ground on Highland Avenue, dim and smoky, but sports a good jukebox. Down Hollywood Boulevard is the **Frolic Room** (6245 Hollywood Blvd., 323-462-5890, 12 pm-2 am). It may very well have the most beautiful neon bar sign in Los Angeles, which appears often in movies. Inside, the fading wallpaper has Al Hirshfeld images of bygone celebrities. Your entrance to the **Smog Cutter** (864 N. Virgil Ave., 323-660-4626, 12 pm -2 am) is somewhat impeded by the pool table. But the Smog Cutter isn't known for its pool, wood paneling, stale smell, or impatient bartenders. It's a local karaoke fave, despite the fact there's no stage, the machine is little, and there's always a line— everybody lines up to sing and everybody has a good time.

VELVET ROPES

Hollywood is home to a race of Beautiful People whose perfect teeth gleam from luscious lips or rugged jaw lines, whose hair shines because it's highlighted ten different colors, whose perfect bodily assets are shown off in designer duds. There's the BPs, whom Nature and Fortune have graced, and then there are those who have achieved the look with a little help. You'll find the BP, and those who want to either be like them or just bask in their reflected glory, behind the velvet ropes. **Deep** (1707 N. Vine St., Hollywood, 323-462-1144, Thurs 9 pm-2 am; Fri-Sat, 8 pm-2 am, reservations suggested for restaurant) is known for the couples it has strategically placed in recesses behind the bar—performing the 21st Century version of go-go dancing, which is simulated intercourse. On weekends you're guaranteed access if you have dinner reservations; otherwise, the line snakes down the block. If the doorman doesn't recognize you or think you rate, you'll need an awfully large bill to convince him. In *addition* to the cover. Ditto the **Sunset Room** (1430 N. Cahuenga Blvd., Hollywood, 323-463-0004, Wed-Sat, 9 pm-2 am, cover), which has a restaurant, bar and dance floor. White tablecloths and gracious service belie how rockin' this place can get. It's one of the only places in the city with a dress code (no jeans or T's) and folks go all out with their get-ups. The original **Hollywood Canteen** (1006 Seward St., Hollywood, 323-465-0961 Mon 11:30 pm-3 am; Tue-Fri 11:30 pm-2 am; Sat 6 pm-3 am) opened during WWII. As thanks for serving their country, founder Bette Davis and her actor pals would serve the GIs nice meals and cocktails. Now, the Canteen has reopened and gone upscale. If you get beyond the velvet rope, you'll find yourself in an airy room whose roof is white tent canvas. Over to the side is an Airstream trailer; inside it's decked out in red and leopard, and is a popular make-out place when it hasn't been reserved for the evening. Inside the bar proper, one shark swims alone in the tank behind the model that takes your drink order. **Barfly** (8730 Sunset Blvd., West Hollywood, 310-360-9490, 7:30 pm-2 am) on Sunset Strip is a bar, disco, and restaurant whose DJs keep it loud and fast, and whose older male clientele in suits and gold chains say in all seriousness: *Who's your Daddy?* You may have to grease the rope-ape's hand to gain access even if you're a hottie, but once inside it's unlikely you'll pay for even one cocktail. It's an unwritten law that women wear sequined halter-tops.

SINGLES SCENE

Any bar can be a "singles" scene, of course, but some are better at it than others. This is exactly what you'll find in Los Feliz's **Good Luck Bar** (1514 Hillhurst Ave., LA, 323-666-3524, Mon-Fri 7 pm-2 am; Sat-Sun 8 pm-2 am). The double-sided bar is centered in a small room, so you can see who's enjoying a cocktail across from you. A keyhole doorway leads into the second room, where low ottomans and couches invite lounging. Down Sunset in Silverlake, you'll find **4100 Bar** (4100 Sunset Blvd., 323-666-4460) which the locals call the **Manzanita Room**, an earlier name that corresponds to its street address. Here, a giant gold Buddha watches over you from the back and the walls are covered with silk tapestries. The sides are lined with benches fronted by tables and chairs, making crowding, on a good night, an advantage for those seeking to make a love connection: leaning in to hear your potential date's conversation is vital because the DJ plays it loud.

HIPSTER HANGOUTS

The **Formosa Café** (7156 Santa Monica Blvd., West Hollywood, 323-850-9050, Mon-Fri 4 pm-2 am; Sat-Sun 6 pm-2 am) on Melrose has a downstairs outdoor bar and upstairs patio/smoking area that have recently been added to this Hollywood landmark. The red booths and walls covered with celebrity photos was featured in *LA Confidential*. The Formosa has a slightly younger and rockin' crowd than that across the street at **Jones**, but the two tend to share clientele. The Asian theme is further exemplified by **Temple Bar** (1026 Wilshire

Blvd, Santa Monica, 310-393-6611, 6 pm-2 am) in terms of décor and multi-ethnic appetizers; a slightly more mixed crowd, in terms of age, tends to hang here, and the place is known for its extensive list of martinis. **The Room** (1626 N. Cahuenga Blvd., 323-462-7196, 8 pm-2 am) in Hollywood and **The Room SM** (1323 Santa Monica Blvd., 310-458-0707, Tues-Sun 8 pm -2 am) in Santa Monica are hard to find, so when you land in either one, you can be sure your drinking companions are equally hip. You must walk down a dumpster-filled alley behind Cahuenga Blvd. in Hollywood to find the unmarked door into The Room, but inside the incense-filled place is a long bar and a DJ spinning an eclectic variety, depending on the night. Hidden as well as The Room, The Room SM is unmarked, and you know you're near the entrance when you're looking at a parking area. While you're down at the beach, you'll want to check out **The Brig** (1515 Abbot Kinney, 310-399-7537, Sun-Thu 6 pm-2 am; Fri-Sat 7 pm-2 am) in Venice, recently refurbished from a dive to a hipster hang. The pool table supports friendly rivalries, and the crowd, while just as accomplished as the scenesters in Hollywood, is much more mellow. Back in Hollywood, on the commercial side of Cahuenga, across a few walls from The Room, you'll find **Beauty Bar**, (1638 N. Cahuenga Blvd., 323-464-7676, Thu-Fri opens at 6; Sat-Wed opens at 8) which you may know from its manifestations in both San Francisco and New York. This is a stylized replica of a beauty parlor from the late '50s/early '60s, and at Happy Hour you can get a manicure while you sip a martini the color of Prell. Old-fashioned hooded dryers line the walls, leading to the smoking room. The crowd is so fashion-forward it's hard to tell whether it's thrift or designer being shown off, but everybody is very friendly. Across the street is **The Burgundy Room**, (1621-1/2 N. Cahuenga Blvd., 323-465-7530, 8 pm-2 am) where intimacy is enforced because if you're not sitting at the bar, you're pressed against the person who is. If you're really good (or really bad) the bartender will light the bar on fire for you. Only at Silverlake's **Akbar** (4356 W. Sunset Blvd., 323-665-6810) will Beau the barkeep rival this act actually *breathing* fire, using Bacardi 151 as fuel. This place is known for being a "mixed" bar—which some take to mean the straights invading a gay hang… or vice versa… Whatever the sexual preference of the patrons, they tend toward the fun and arty. In Echo Park you'll come upon the **Short Stop**, (1455 Sunset Blvd., 213-482-4942, 4 pm-2 am) announced merely with small neon "Cocktails." Once the off-duty headquarters of the famously corrupt Rampart Division cops, the Short Stop is now "San Frangeles" central—all the recent transplants escaping San Francisco's dead economy have found a similar geography to inhabit in Silverlake and Echo Park, and turned the bar into their local. Spacious, it sports a billiards room, the bar area with original gun lockers, and a dance floor rimmed with small tables and crowned by a disco ball. The Short Stop also has a terrific Happy Hour. Over the hill, deep in Silverlake, you'll find **The Roost** (3100 Los Feliz Blvd., 323-664-7272, 10 am-2 am) and down the way a piece, **Bigfoot Lodge** (3172 Los Feliz Blvd., 323-662-9227, 8 pm-2 am). The Roost boasts a bar that seems to be a porch, and the highlight of its décor is the wagon wheels. Gangs of same-sex friends congregate here and enjoy free bags of popcorn and after a libation or two start to mix it up with each other and the blue-collar workers who also find the place enticing. Bigfoot Lodge is known for its Rockabilly guys and gals (as well as the occasional booze-induced Bigfoot sighting). Rockabillies and lounge aficionados populate **The Derby** (4500 Los Feliz Blvd., 323-663-8979, www.the-derby.com) and **The Dresden Room** (1760 N. Vermont, 323-665-4294, Mon-Sat 11:30 am-3:30 pm; Sat 4:30 pm -2 am; Sunday 4-10 pm). The Derby sports a piano bar, lounge, and dance floor, and free swing dancing lessons (call for times) and has recently branched out to include Alternative Rock one or two nights per week. Dancing, as your mom always told you (or should have), is a great way to meet people, as is the open-mike night at The Dresden. Local legends and lounge act Marty and Elayne, who have reigned for nearly two decades, are the primary draw; but so are the very friendly waitresses and the traditional décor, which appeared in the movie *Swingers*. If Hollywood still beckons you, try the **Lava Lounge** (1533 N. La Brea Ave., 323-876-6612, 9 pm-2 am) located in the middle of a little strip mall; inside, you seem to be inside the cooled crater of a volcano. Small bar and lethal tropical drinks. Still single after all this bar hoppin'? Try **Daddy's** (1610 N. Vine St., Hollywood, 323-463-7777) where the primary lighting is via candles; it's so dim that if you think you've seen a movie actor you can't really be certain, but you usually are. Daddy's boasts a trendy crowd, and is packed on the weekends; sometimes you'll meet people just by waiting in line.

You've done the singles scene, and you've met someone— or several someones—who appear promising. Check out **Bar Marmont** (8171 Sunset Blvd., West Hollywood, 323-650-0575) located at the base of the famous Chateau. On the outside it's a grass shack reminiscent of both Tiki Ti and the Silverlake Lounge, but inside it's all elegance. Butterflies are suspended here and there, the atmo is relaxed and inviting; the famous martinis are produced with a flourish, and served with an adorable little pitcher on ice. You have an impression of being in a dusky outdoors, belied only by the inviting furniture. The staff treats everybody with equal courtesy and a special attention which indicates you're an A-list actor, whether or not you actually are. Or head east on Sunset past Vine to **The Well** (6255 Sunset Blvd., 323-467-9355, Mon-Fri 5 pm-2 am; Sat 8 pm-2 am; Sun 9 pm-2 am. Entrance on Argyle) which rapidly achieved an honored status among local cocktail devotees. What makes The Well special is the variety of the crowd. While the décor might lead you to expect a bunch of lawyers or professionals, the patrons are actually a variety of sophisticates drawn from all of Hollywood's subsets. Now get out there and join 'em.

Hey, kids! Don't drink and drive. Write this number down, and stick it in your wallet: **United Independent Taxi**, 1-800-308-0700. Concerned about what to wear? A black leather jacket, neat jeans, and nice shoes work well at most places. Always carry an ID. And cash: it's required at the dive bars, and it makes everybody's life easier everywhere else.

EMERGENCY AND HEALTH LA

Police, Fire, Ambulance (Emergency): 911

Poison Control Center: 800-876-4766, 24 hour

AIDS Information Hotline: 800-922-AIDS

Child Protective Services: 323-766-2345

Rape and Battery Hotline: 310-392-8391 (West Side) 213-626-3393 (Central LA)

Alcoholics Anonymous: 323-936-4343

Narcotics Anonymous: 323-933-5395

Red Cross Disaster Services: 213-739-5200, 24 hour

LA Free Clinic (8084 Beverly Blvd., West Hollywood, 323-653-1990. Under 18: 6043 Hollywood Blvd., 323-462-4158) Sexually transmitted diseases, flu shots, dental care, general health care. Call for appointment, no walk-ins.

Optometric Center of Los Angeles (3916 S. Broadway, LA, 323-234-9137) Clinical facility. Basic eye exam starts at $30, tests and screening for eye diseases, low-cost glasses.

LA County / USC Medical Center (1200 State St., LA, 323-442-8500) Emergency and trauma care, psychiatric services, neo-natal, general health care.

TO LOS ANGELES

Schrader Gay and Lesbian Center (1625 N. Schrader Blvd., Hollywood, main line: 323-993-7570, clinic: 323-993-7500) STD and HIV testing; pap smears; gynecological; transgender, gay and lesbian support groups; a youth shelter; counseling; mammograms. Spanish spoken, fees on a sliding scale.

Hollywood-Sunset Free Clinic (3324 Sunset Blvd., 323-660-5715) General medical care, family planning and birth control, STD and HIV testing, mammograms. All services provided on a donations-only basis.

Planned Parenthood LA (Hollywood, Burbank, East LA, Canoga Park, Pomona, Santa Monica, Lawndale, Van Nuys, and Whittier. For a nearby location, call 323-226-0800 or 818-843-2009.) STD and HIV testing, prenatal care, family planning, condoms, Norplant, birth control pills, cervical caps, diaphragms, breast exams, male/female sterilizations, hormone therapy, pregnancy tests, emergency contraceptives. Fees are on a sliding scale, Spanish spoken.

LA ON FOUR LEGS

Here are some good resources for pet owners in Los Angeles:

ANIMAL EMERGENCY FACILITY (1736 Sepulveda, south of Santa Monica Blvd., West LA, 310-473-1561, 24 hours) This awesome hospital not only offers around-the-clock emergency care, they also have vets that keep regular office hours. But this isn't just an animal ER—they have specialists and miracle-working surgeons that go above and beyond treatment at a neighborhood animal hospital. They saved my kitty Beigey-Brown, who had a collapsed lung among other complications. Okay, so it wasn't cheap… but two years later, she's running around like it never happened and I still think it was the best "purr-chase" I ever made!

ANIMAL EMERGENCY CENTER (11740 Ventura Blvd., Studio City, 818-760-3882, open 5 pm-8:30 am weekdays, and 24 hours on weekends) This small hospital has a caring staff of vets available to treat "after-hours" animal emergencies, from simple mishaps to major accidents.

VETERINARY MEDICAL CENTER OF STUDIO CITY (11723 Ventura Blvd., Studio City, 818-762-3111) Dr. Steve Aboulafia and staff are friendly and compassionate, taking care of everything from shots and routine check-ups to surgery. They also offer feline and canine dental care, spaying, neutering, boarding, and a few different lines of restricted diet specialty foods. Pet adoptions are held Saturday afternoons from noon to 3 p.m. Charlie, the feline answer to George Clooney on *ER* is a foxy white kitty with a bedside manner (and the run of the place) that lounges on top of the admissions desk, checking out the incoming patients.

GATEWAY ANIMAL HOSPITAL (431 West Los Feliz Blvd., LA, 323-256-5840) A small full-service hospital that accepts city-sponsored spaying and neutering coupons.

VETMOBILE (310-412-7000) They will take your pet to the doctor when you can't.

FIFI AND ROMEO (7282 Beverly Blvd., W. Hollywood, 323-857-7215) A whimsical, frivolous pet accessories store. Need a rhinestone collar, a doggie sweater, or gourmet treats?

AQUARIUM STOCK COMPANY (8070 Beverly Blvd., LA, 323-653-8930) All sorts of freshwater and saltwater aquarium supplies, tropical fish, birds, reptiles, and everything you need to feed or house them. This place has been in business since

1948 and you could lose hours just staring at all the crazy creatures.

PETCO (www.petco.com) Locations all over Los Angeles. Open seven days — pet supplies and food, aquariums and fish, birds, small reptiles, varying by location. Some stores offer grooming and vaccination clinics as well.

BRONSON CANYON PARK (Bronson Ave. north of Franklin, Hollywood, park closes at sunset) Drive up past the picnic tables to the last parking lot. Park your car; grab a leash for Rover, and head to your left, up the dirt road. A few feet along, you can let your doggie off the leash (like everyone else does—technically you're not supposed to) and hike through the canyon until you get up to the Bat Caves. Yup, this crazy rock formation of three cave-like tunnels is the real location of the exterior of the Bat Cave from 1960s TV series *Batman*. It's also been featured in a ton of movies, everything from early "B" Westerns to *Short Cuts*. Dogs love sniffing around up here, but even if you don't have a dog, you will, too.

AUTO EROTIC

Everything you've heard about a car being an absolute necessity in Los Angeles is true. Over the past few years, there have been many improvements in public transportation but having wheels at your disposal will make your life *much* easier. If you're not used to driving in LA, you should know that all of those clichés and horror stories are true as well. Traffic is consistently insane: people eat, babble on cell phones, apply make-up, flirt with other drivers, blow red lights, make u-turns at random, and barely ever bother to signal. As far as most people are concerned, a yellow light means "Drive as fast as you can." Be forewarned, all you wannabe street-rodders: many intersections have those infamous cameras that will photograph you cruising through a red light, and then send you an astronomical ticket. Rush hour gridlock and road rage are a fact of everyday life. But gruesome as it may sound, there are days when traffic flows smoothly, it's sunny, you're on your way to the beach, and driving in LA is great. A few words to the wise: read posted signs *carefully* before parking—the notorious Parking Enforcement assholes (job requirements are, in no particular order: having a scary hairdo, a big fat butt, and a bad attitude) would like nothing better than to give you a ticket. Sometimes paying an exorbitant valet parking fee may be more financially sound than driving around looking for a space on the street! Also, in California, car insurance is mandatory. You can get your license suspended if you don't have it. And it's probably a good idea to join AAA (www.csaa.com), they'll bring you gas, jump-start your car, or provide four free tows a year if you get stranded someplace. Always lock your car, and try not to leave anything valuable in it.

LA always has been — and always will be — a place that worships at the Altar of the Auto, so here are some places that'll help you feel the love:

HOLLYWOOD SPRING AND AXEL (6009 W. Sunset, Hollywood, 323-464-4051) This place looks like a set from *The Fast and The Furious,* a true old-school garage. There are engines, tires, and vintage auto hulks lying around, a (friendly) pitbull on a chain, and grease-stained pin-ups of racecars and foxy chicks lining the walls. Honest, fast, inexpensive service, and gear head extraordinaire maniac/mechanic Chris Doyle is GOD. Really. I actually got on my hands and knees and kowtowed to him in the middle of the street once, because he has saved my ass – and my '64 Comet Caliente – so many times.

AUTO ZONE (Citywide - many locations - www.autozone.com) A great place to go for new parts and tools if you do home repairs, or to pick up oil, transmission fluid, car wax, etc. Other similar stores with multiple locations include **Chief Auto Parts** and **Pep Boys**.

PETERSON AUTO MUSEUM (6060 Wilshire Blvd., LA, 323-930-CARS, admission: $7, seniors/students: $5, under 12: $3) The museum features cars as art. Past shows have included movie vehicles, souped-up hot rods, vintage autos, and wildly decorated custom Low Rider cars.

DREAMBOATS (12333 W. Pico Blvd., LA, 310-828-3014) The place to go if you wanna make like a movie star and rent some styley wheels (like a cherried-out '30s gangster sedan or '57 Chevy convertible) for a special occasion. At $350 a day, it isn't cheap, but if you got the dough, go for it.

THOMAS TOPS (1317 Caheunga Blvd., Hollywood, 323-469-3277) If you need to get a convertible roof redone, this is the place to go. They also do auto interiors, car covers and even boats. They are reliable and work quickly.

JERRY'S GARAGE (1645 N. Gower, Hollywood; 323-464-7381) A small, all-service garage that does routine maintenance and major repairs on everything from domestic and foreign cars to news vans. Honest, affordable work and the staff are all nice people.

BAYLESS CHEVRON (1869 Hillhurst Ave., Los Feliz, 323-662-1360) Another full-service family garage, as well as a gas station. I have to apologize to the staff for mentioning this, but what makes this place really interesting in a macabre way is that the Manson Family used this service station as a pit stop. After murdering Leno and Rosemary LaBianca, at their nearby Los Feliz home, the Family came here to rinse the blood off their hands and dump their bloody clothes. Hence, (probably much to the owner's chagrin) many locals refer to this garage as "Leno LaBianca Chevron."

THE BLESSING OF THE CARS (www.blessingofthecars.com)
If you like cars and you happen to be in the LA area during the
last week of July, you MUST attend this bash, your mind will
be blown. Run by the ultra-hip husband and wife team Gabriel
and Stephanie Baltierra, BOTC is an annual all-day event featuring a vintage car and motorcycle show, contests with prizes
for things like "Best Flames," and "Best Street Rod." There
are booths with auto accessories, new and used parts and accessories, specialty car magazines and books, car-themed
T-shirts, and food. People-watching is prime too, with a bunch
of cute grease monkeys and Betty Page-looking chicks running around showing off their tattoos in skimpy sun dresses
Bands play all day long, there's usually a pinstriping or detail-
ing demonstration, auto-themed art, and '50s hot rod movies
being screened. Oh, and of course there's a Catholic priest on
hand (dressed in checkered, racing-striped vestments) to bless
your vehicle.

POMONA AUTO SWAP MEET (Held every six weeks, Sun.
5 am-2 pm, Los Angeles County Fairplex, 1101 W. McKinley,
Pomona, 909-623-3711) You won't believe this swap meet. It
stretches almost as far as the eye can see. Dealers from all over
California and neighboring states bring cars to buy and sell.
From perfectly restored vintage vehicles to frightening clunkers,
from seats to upholstery buttons, nitro-blasting hot rods to
Model T-s, as well as the odd Airstream trailer, dirt bikes, kiddie
toy cars, motorcycles, old racing trophies, antique Schwinn
bicycles, auto magazines, racing leathers, T-shirts, coveralls,
chrome parts and logos, you name it. Dreaming of a fully restored 1932 Highboy or a lime green metal flake pimpmobile
with a faux-fur interior and the signs of the zodiac decorating
the steering wheel? If you can't find it here, it probably doesn't
exist. Bargaining is a must. Make sure to bring sunblock, wa-

ter and cold, hard cash. If you're looking for a used car and don't feel like waiting for the Swap Meet, pick up a copy of *The Recycler* or *Photo Buys* (available at newsstands and convenience stores, every Thursday) and try your luck with the extensive used auto listings.

THAT'S ENTERTAINMENT!

CITY CELEBRATIONS

This is by no means a complete list, but certain yearly events are tons of fun, and usually free. Here are a few of the better ones...

January

The Tournament of Roses Parade. New Year's Day, Pasadena. 626-795-4171. Amazing to see — and smell — in real life. All the floats are made out of flowers. Standing or sitting in the street is free, but the good spots fill up the night before: prepare to camp out.

February

African-American History Month Celebrations: many citywide, check papers for info, locations, and schedule.

TO LOS ANGELES

Chinese New Year Celebration. 323-617-0396. The Golden Dragon Parade, a carnival, crafts, food, and, of course, the LA Miss Chinatown Contest.

March
Blessing of the Animals. El Pueblo de Los Angeles (125 Paseo de la Plaza, Downtown LA, 323-628-7833.) Total pandemonium (and lots of flying fur) as people flock to this free event to get their pets blessed by Catholic priests.

LA Marathon. 310-444-5544. Great for the runners and cyclists, but if you're trying to go anywhere before 4 p.m., forget it! Free to all who wish to watch or participate.

April
Earth Day. 800-439-4666. This number provides info on the various celebrations or volunteer/participant activities, as well as other numbers for environmental or sanitation issues.

May
Cinco De Mayo Festival. El Pueblo de Los Angeles, 323-625-5045. Slightly smaller and a little more focused on cultural heritage than Fiesta Broadway, celebrate with Aztec and Ballet Folklorico dancers, roving mariachis, carnival rides and games, face-painting, and of course, tacos and lots of beer!

June
Irish Fair. Santa Anita Racetrack, Arcadia, 626-574-7223. This isn't free, but if you plan on going, designate a non-drinking driver — it's wild! Irish music, step dancing, Gaelic sports, a medieval Irish village, horse show, and LOTS of beer and Irish whiskey.

Gay and Lesbian Pride Celebration. Santa Monica Blvd. and West Hollywood Park, check papers for times, events and performers. An amazing parade full of drag cheerleading squads and the awesome Dykes on Bikes, a carnival, info booths, bands, and a city full of queer and queer-friendly folks celebrating like mad. Usually the third weekend in June.

July

Fourth of July Fireworks Displays check papers for citywide info.

Dance Kaleidoscope. A citywide festival featuring performances of ballet, modern, tap, ethnic, jazz & more. Check papers for performance times and locations. Incredible and very affordable — hot new companies and choreographers.

The Lotus Festival. Echo Park Lake, Downtown LA, 323-485-8744. Celebrate Asian/Pacific Rim cultures with dragon boat races, a flower show, ethnic food, kids activities, various shows of music and dance.

August

African Marketplace and Cultural Fair. Rancho La Cienega Park, Crenshaw District, 323-290-3141. Music, dancing, mask-making, African-American crafts, yummy foods, clothing booths, fortune-telling, hair-weaving, live entertainment.

Watts Summer Festival. 323-789-7304. A weeklong festival with art exhibits, crafts, food booths, community information, and sports.

September

LA County Fair. Pomona Sportsplex, 909-623-3111. Definitely worth the 40-minute drive and reasonable admission, this is the world's largest county fair with rides, shows, bands, games, kiddie stuff, tons of food and livestock. See pigs bigger than your sofa! Eat cotton candy! Squaredance!

October

AFI Film Festival. 323-856-7600. One of the biggest film festivals in the US.

West Hollywood Halloween Celebration. 323-848-6308. The entire neighborhood is blocked off, or so it seems! Bands, impromptu parades, drag queens showing their undies, scary people doing scary things — tons o'fun and free. Just be prepared to walk — a lot.

November

Dia De Los Muertos. El Pueblo de Los Angeles, 323-628-3562. Celebrate Day of the Dead, a Mexican tradition: eat sugar skulls, watch Aztec dancers, dress like a skeleton, and swig Tecate and cheap margaritas.

Hollywood Christmas Parade. Hollywood and Sunset Blvds., Thanksgiving Weekend Sunday 6 p.m. Floats, celebrities, marching bands, and Santa. Also a lot of street vendors, inebriated trailer trash, gangbangers and bag people, but always fun. Dress warmly, the event usually lasts over two hours and it does get cold. For the best curbside seating, camp out mid-afternoon and bring a thermos of something toasty to drink.

THEME PARKS and ATTRACTIONS

Call ahead to confirm hours and admission prices!

Knott's Berry Farm (8039 Beach Blvd., Buena Park, 714-220-5200) Open daily except Christmas. Knott's has six areas of exciting rides, live shows, and restaurants, most based on a Wild West theme. They also provide a shuttle from major LA area hotels and offer discounted group rates for 15 or more. Ticket prices: general admission $40, seniors over 60 $30, children 3-11 $30, and children under 2 are free.

TO LOS ANGELES

Six Flags California - Magic Mountain and Hurricane Harbor (Interstate 5, Valencia, 818-367-5965, www.sixflags.com) Located about 40 minutes north of LA, Magic Mountain offers a one-price admission for heart-pounding thrill rides, spine-cracking coasters, concerts, shows, and attractions. Next door is Hurricane Harbor Waterpark (open May-September) - separate admission required. Six Flags opens daily at 10 a.m. during the extended summer months, and weekends and holidays the rest of the year. Ticket prices: general admission $42.99, seniors over 55 and children under 48" $26.99, and children under 2 are free.

Disneyland (Anaheim, 714-781-7290) Mickey Mouse as far as the eye can see. Located about 30 minutes south of downtown LA, Disneyland is the granddaddy of theme parks, spread out over 65 acres with a resort hotel complex. Kiddie rides, thrill rides, live shows, fireworks, roving characters, movies, and virtual attractions, plus guided tours. Open everyday. Hours are generally 10 a.m. to 10 p.m., but may vary so call ahead. Locals know that the park is generally a lot less crowded on overcast, chilly or rainy days, and this really makes a difference in the time you spend waiting in line, so you might want to take that into consideration when you plan your trip. Disneyland does not sell tickets, they sell "passports": regular $45, seniors $43, children 3-9 $35, and children under 3 are free. California residents (with ID) get in for $35. Longer passports for multiple entries are available, too. Disneyland has an entire new adjacent park open as well, called **Disney's California Adventure.** Admission is separate (same as Disneyland rates) and all the rides, attractions and shows have a California theme.

THE UNDERGROUND GUIDE

Sea World (500 Sea World Dr., San Diego, 714-939-6212 - for directions, call 619-226-3901, www.seaworld.com) From Interstate 5 or 8, exit Seaworld Drive and turn west towards the park entrance. Open daily at 10 a.m. (9 during summer). Aquariums, an outdoor stadium with sharks, seals, dolphins, killer whales, polar bears, and more, including Baby Shamu, born in 2001. Five different shows, twenty attractions and exhibits, plus gift shops and a number of restaurants. Single day tickets: adult $42.95, children 3-11 $32.95, and seniors $39.95. Multi-day passes also available.

Universal Studios City Walk and Tour (100 Universal City Plaza, Universal City, 818-622-3801, www.univeralstudios.com) Open daily 9 am-6 pm, 7 pm on weekends. The City Walk has theme-based restaurants, including all things sausage, a beachy fish place, B.B. King's Blues Club, a magic eatery, etc.; a huge megaplex movie theater; the Universal Amphitheater, featuring everything from rock to the Radio City Music Hall Rockettes, and tons of stores. The tour's tram winds through the studio's back lot - see King Kong up close, the *Jaws* shark, the house from *Psycho*, Spiderman and more. Also movie-themed thrill rides: E.T., Shrek, and Jurassic Park (bring yer raincoat for that last one!) Interactive shows, street performers and celeb impersonators for photo-ops. Single day tickets: adult $45, children 3-9 $35, and seniors $34.

NBC Studios Tour (3000 W. Alameda, Burbank, 818-840-3537) Not exactly a theme park, but it's the only television network that gives guided tours and it's ten minutes away from central Hollywood. Visit the *Tonight Show* set, see the sound, special effects, and wardrobe departments, and maybe even get a glimpse of a star! You can also request free *Tonight Show* tickets, available on a first-come, first-served basis, or write ahead and specify the day you wish to be part of the audience.

Hollywood Wax Museum (6767 Hollywood Blvd., Hollywood, 323-462-8860) Open daily from 10 till midnight, 1 a.m. on weekends. This slightly cheesy extravaganza features everything from "The Last Supper" to "The Wizard of Oz" plus all your fave Hollywood stars, old and new. Adults: $10.95, seniors: $8.50, kids 6-12: $6.95, under 6, free. It's also located only about a block from...

Mann's Chinese Theater (6915 Hollywood Blvd., Hollywood), where, for free, you can browse around the courtyard and fit your feet into the footprints of Clark Gable, Marilyn Monroe, the Marx Brothers... heck, even the cast of *Baywatch*! This is also the place to catch various bus tour vans for guided tours through Hollywood - and how could you miss the megamall at Hollywood and Highland, featuring clubs, restaurants, and the brand new home of the Oscars, the **Kodak Theater**.

Ripley's Believe It or Not Museum (6780 Hollywood Blvd., Hollywood, 323-466-6335) This gem of modern schlock features curiosities, ranging from strange to mind-boggling. See a life-sized statue of John Wayne made out of laundry lint, two-headed calves and real shrunken heads. Adults: $10, kids 6-12 $7.95, under 5 free, and discounts of a dollar off admissions for seniors, military personnel and AAA members.

Guiness Book of World Records Museum (6764 Hollywood Blvd., Hollywood, 323-463-6433) More tacky fun discovering the shortest, tallest, fastest, loudest, richest, most tattooed, etc. Crazy facts about humans, natural disasters, science, literature, show business, you name it. Adults: $10.95, seniors: $8.50, kids 6-12: $6.95, under 5, free.

MUSEUMS

** Free once a month or everyday
 * Cheap (under $5) admission

The Autry Museum of Western Heritage (4700 Western Heritage Way, Griffith Park, 323-667-2000) Closed Monday open 10 am-5 pm; $7.50, $5 seniors & students, $3 children ages 2 to 12.

*__Cabrillo Marine Aquarium__ (3720 Stephen White Dr., San Pedro, 310-548-7562) Open Tues-Fri noon-5 pm, Sat-Sun 10 am- 5 pm, $2, suggested donation for adults, $1 children & seniors.

**__California African-American Museum__ (600 State Dr., Exposition Park, 213-744-7432) Open Tues-Sun 10 am-5 pm, free.

**__California Science Center__ (formerly the Museum of Science and Industry, 700 State Dr., Exposition Park, 213-744-7400) Open daily, 10 am-5 pm, free.

**__Getty Center__ (1200 Getty Center Dr., West LA, 310-440-7300) Open Sat-Sun, 10 am-6 pm, Tues-Wed, 11 am-7 pm, Thurs-Fri, 11 am-9 pm, free but parking ($5) reservations are required.

*__Grier Musser Antiques Museum__ (403 S. Bonnie Brae St., 213-413-1814) Wed-Fri, noon-4 pm; Sat 11 am-4 pm; $5 adults, $3 children & seniors. Call ahead.

TO LOS ANGELES

Hollywood Entertainment Museum (7021 Hollywood Blvd., 323-465-7900) Closed Wednesday, open 11 am-6 pm; $7.50, $3 children, under 5 free.

**Huntington Library, Art Collections, and Botanical Gardens (1151 Oxford Road, San Marino, 626-405-2141) Open Tues-Fri, noon-4:30 pm; Sat-Sun 10:30 am-4:30 pm. $10, $8.50 seniors, $5 students & children, under 12 free. Free admission the first Thursday of every month.

Japanese American National Museum (369 E. First St., 213-625-0414) Open Tues-Wed, Fri-Sun, 10 am-5 pm, Thurs, 10 am-8 pm, $6, $5 seniors, $3 students & children over 5.

**Korean Cultural Center (5505 Wilshire Blvd., 323-936-7141) Open Mon-Fri 10 am-5 pm, Sat 10 am-1 pm, free.

Los Angeles Children's Museum (Two new facilities, opening 2004)

**Los Angeles County Museum of Art (5905 Wilshire Blvd., 323-857-6000) Open Mon., Tues. & Thurs., noon-8 p.m.; Fri., noon-9 p.m., Sat.-Sun., 11 a.m.-8 p.m.; $7, $5 students & seniors over 62, $1 ages 6 to 17, children 5 under free. Free admission the second Tuesday of every month.

**Museum of Contemporary Art (250 S. Grand Ave., 213-626-6222) Open Fri.-Sun. & Tues.-Wed., 11 am-5 pm; Thurs., 11 am-8 pm; $8, $5 seniors & students, members & children under 12 free. Free admission every Thursday 5-8 pm.

**Museum of Jurassic Technology (9341 Venice Blvd., West LA) Thursdays from 2-8 pm; Fridays, Saturdays and Sundays from Noon - 6 p.m. Suggested donations: adults, $4; seniors, students, and children 12 to 21, $2.50; under 12, free. Free admission after 7:45 on Thursdays and 5:45 on Friday, Saturday, and Sunday.

***Museum of Latin American Art** (628 Alamitos Ave., Long Beach, 562- 437-1689) Open Tues.-Sat., 11:30 a.m.-7:30 p.m.; Sun., noon-6 p.m.; $5, $3 seniors, children under 12 free.

****Museum of Neon Art/MONA** (501 W. Olympic at Hope St., 213-489-9918.) Open Wed.-Sun., noon-5 p.m.; $5, $3.50 students & seniors; free 2nd Thursday evening of every month.

Museum of Television & Radio (465 N. Beverly Dr., Beverly Hills, 310-786-1000) Open Wed.-Sun., noon-5 p.m.; Thurs. till 8 p.m.; $6, $4 students & seniors, $3 children under 13.

Museum of Tolerance (9786 W. Pico Blvd., 310-553-9036) Open Mon.-Thurs., 11:30 a.m.-4 p.m.; Fri., 10 a.m.-1 p.m.; Sun., 10 a.m.-5 p.m.; tours take approximately 2 hours; reservations recommended; closed Sat.; $9, $7 seniors 62 & up, $5.50 students, $3 children ages 3-12.

****Natural History Museum** (900 Exposition Blvd., Exposition Park, 213-763-DINO) Open Mon.-Fri., 9:30 a.m.-5 p.m., Sat.-Sun., 11 a.m.-5 p.m.; $8, $5.50 seniors & students over 12, $2 children ages 5 to 12, children under 5 free; Free admission the first Tuesday of every month.

***Norton Simon Museum of Art** (411 W. Colorado Blvd., Pasadena, 626-449-6840) Open Wed.-Sun., noon-6 p.m.; $6, $3 seniors & students, children under 12, students under 18 and members free.

TO LOS ANGELES

Pacific Asia Museum (46 N. Los Robles Ave., Pasadena, 626-449-2742) Open Wed.-Sun., 10 a.m.-5 p.m.; $5, $3 seniors & students, children 12 & under free; free admission on the third Saturday of each month.

Page Museum at the La Brea Tar Pits (5801 Wilshire Blvd., 323-857-6311) Open Tues.-Sun., 10 a.m.-5 p.m.; $6, $3.50 students (ages 12-17) & seniors, $2 children ages 5-12, under 5 free; Free admission the first Tuesday of every month.

Pepperdine University Frederick R. Weisman Museum of Art (24255 Pacific Coast Highway, 310-456-4851) Closed Monday, open 11 a.m.-5 p.m.; free.

*Santa Monica Museum of Art** (Bergamot Station, 2525 Michigan Ave., 310-586-6488) Open Tues.-Sat., 11 a.m.-6 p.m.; $3 suggested donation, $2 students, seniors & artists.

Skirball Cultural Center (2701 N. Sepulveda Blvd., 310-440-4500) Closed Monday, open noon-5 p.m.; Sun., 11 a.m.-5 p.m.; $8, $6 students & seniors, children under 12 free.

*Southwest Museum** (234 Museum Dr., 323-221-2164) Closed Monday, open 10 a.m.-5 p.m.; $5, $3 seniors & students, $2 ages 7-18, children under 6 free.

UCLA Fowler Museum of Cultural History (310-825-4361) Open Wed.-Sun., noon-5 p.m.; Thurs., noon-8 p.m.; free.

USC Fisher Gallery (823 Exposition Blvd., 213-740-4561) Open Tues.-Fri., noon-5 p.m.; Sat., 11 a.m.-3 p.m.; free.

NOT FOR KIDS ONLY
S.A. Griffin

Contrary to some popular opinions, Los Angeles and its environs can actually be kid-friendly. As a dad with a growing boy, countless hours have been spent with my son doing the things that I will be hipping you to in this little section. If possible, visit these places on weekdays, as weekends are a beehive of tourists and locals alike. As in most big cities, always watch your back, hide all valuables in the trunk of your car (this is a big one, and do it BEFORE you drive to your destination so you don't forget), and walk with your purse on the inside. There is a rich and diverse amalgam of activities for the younger set besides the usual Disneyland-type stuff. Most of these places are fairly inexpensive or free, and are for the entire family.

Griffith Park (www.ci.la.ca.us/RAP/grifmet/gp/index.htm), a true Southern California showpiece, rates as one of the grandest parks anywhere on the planet. At 4,218 acres, it is one of the largest parks of its kind in the world and the biggest in the U.S. It has a number of entrances, the most accessible being right at the corner of Los Feliz Blvd. and Riverside Drive, adjacent to the **William Mulholland Memorial Fountain**. During the day it's a fountain, but at night, holy-hole-in-a-donut Batman!, it's a Technicolor spectacle! Fabulous changing colors and dancing waters, Liberace would've loved it. It's one of my wife's favorite things in LA, and she's from Jersey so it's gotta be worthwhile cheese. Aside from being a favorite picnic spot during the week and especially on weekends, Griffith Park has many fun things to offer kids and adults alike. Included within the boundaries of this wonderful park are a boy's and girl's camp, a golf course, 28 tennis courts, and the world-famous Hollywood sign. Beware the drum circles on Sundays (or join in, if you like). Parking is free except during events at the Greek Theater. The following are all located within the park's parameters.

The **Griffith Park Merry-Go-Round** is a real park treasure. Owned and operated by Warren Deasy, it was built in 1926 for the Spreckles family at North Tonawanda, New York because it was close to the Erie Canal for easy shipping. Created originally to be used at the San Diego Pier, sadly shut down because of the Great Depression of 1929, the carousel then did a brief stint in Balboa Park and then moved to its present location at Griffith Park in 1937. Legend has it that Walt Disney used to bring his daughters here to ride the painted ponies, and while they were having their fun, Walt would sit on the green bench to watch. Guess that Walt decided he wanted one of his own for the amusement of his girls, and with the help of the Davis family who owned the carousel at the time, indeed purchased his own. The city of Burbank and Glendale didn't want it (too 'carnie'), so Walt bought real estate in Anaheim to house his ride, and the rest, as they say, is history. My wife and I had our wedding under the big oak tree nearby, and then invited everyone to join us on the merry-go-round to begin our new life together. Rides $1. Open 11 a.m. - 5 p.m. weekends and everyday during the summer and all school holidays.

The **Autry Museum of Western Heritage** (323-667-2000). Check out the crooning celluloid cowboy's museum. Many fine exhibits and regular features including touring musical acts and cowboy poetry. The **Golden Spur Cafe** offers Western fare and a recorded voice on the phone machine says they have some of the best chili around. Hmmmm… Open Tuesday-Sunday, 10a.m.-5p.m. Admission is $7.50 for adults, students and seniors over 60 $5, children 2-12 $3, children under 2 are free. Closed Mondays, Thanksgiving and Christmas. Free second Tuesday of every month.

The **Greek Theater** (323-665-1927). Very cool outdoor amphitheater closed winter through early spring. Bring a jacket, even in summer. Call for shows and prices. Like most concert events, the parking is a real idiot ballet and costs, so if you can, get here early and bring a picnic. Get tanked beforehand and save some bread 'cause the cheap drinks aren't cheap. Saw the amazing Tony Bennett here once upon a time with a full orchestra, the entire stage bathed in pink light. Hey, it doesn't get much better than that.

Travel Town (323-662-9678) Free. Over 40 antique trains and locomotives on display year-round for climbing and looking. Antique autos and fire engines. Miniature train rides for the little ones. Live steam trains on Saturdays. Birthday parties on old trains - call for info.

LA Zoo (323-644-6400) Open everyday but Christmas, 10 a.m.-5 p.m. They put the critters to bed by 4:30. Admission: over 12 years, $8.25; children 2-12, $3.25; over 65, $5.25; children under 2 are free. Get on the tram for $3 and save your feet. Bring your own food, as the chow is overpriced and not very good. Actually it's pretty lousy, but the kids might enjoy the french fries shaped like lions and tigers and bears, oh my!

The **Griffith Observatory** (323-664-1191) Sad to say, the observatory will be closed for renovation/expansion and is scheduled to reopen on May 14, 2005 on the 70th anniversary. To find out what's up you can call the number above or visit online at www.griffithobservatory.org. Gonna miss the Tesla Coil exhibit.

Pony Ride (323-664-3266) Inexpensive, safe, and gentle pony rides for tiny tots, plus an old-fashioned wagon ride for the whole family. After the kids have had their fun on the equines, then jump on board the... **Miniature Train Ride** (323-664-6788) a working small-scale train that takes you through the park. Both of these cheap and fun activities are located just inside the entrance at Los Feliz and Riverside. Buy your tickets at the small but lively gift shop.

When you leave Griffith Park, if you are looking for someplace to eat, roll on down to the **House of Pies** (1869 N. Vermont Ave., 323-666-9961, 6:30 a.m. - 1 a.m.). Located at the corner of Vermont and Franklin Avenues in lovely Los Feliz (according to *Vogue* magazine, one of the hippest neighborhoods in all of LA, or as they put it, the "left coast," but puh-leeze!). The food is cheap, edible, and true to the name, they have a great assortment of pies. A neighborhood hang with an eclectic mix of folks where breakfast is the best fare of the day. The friendly staff makes this a very pleasant respite for the whole fam-damily before or after visiting the park. When you are finished with your repast, the teens and like-minded boho-hipsters will enjoy the shops and boutiques that line Vermont Ave. between Hollywood Blvd. and Franklin Ave. It is a safe and easy walk.

If you like movies in the grand tradition of film, then you owe it to yourself and your family to visit the glorious **El**

Capitan Theater (6838 Hollywood Blvd., 323-467-7674, http://cms.disney.go.com/disneypictures/el_capitan/) in the heart of Hollywood, and/or the **Alex Theater** (216 N. Brand Blvd., 800-414-2539; www.geocities.com/bijoumanager/Alex-theater.html) in Glendale. Both spectacular theaters are completely restored and well worth the price of admission. The El Capitan debuted in 1926 as Hollywood's "First Home of Spoken Drama." Catch the El Capitan during the release of a new Disney flick. The prices are higher, but you get a great live show before the movie, which includes dancing and singing Disney characters. I've taken my son to several of these and there is nothing like it. Highly recommended! The Alex Theater began its life as a silent movie house in 1925 and is among other things, the home of The Gay Men's Chorus of Los Angeles (www.gmcla.org/Pages/alex.html). You can catch movies, road shows and other wonderful events here. Call for times and prices.

For a completely different movie experience, check out the giant **Imax Theater** (700 State Dr., 213-774-2014, www.casciencectr.org), at the corner of Figueroa and Exposition in downtown Los Angeles. The Imax Theater is a real family movie-going experience in front of a screen five stories tall with a six-channel Surround Sound system. The films are spectacular, top-notch G-rated flicks in a documentary format, but don't let that throw ya, it is really a lot of fun. Call for films, times, and admission.

When you're done with the movies, walk next door to either the **California Science Center** (700 State Dr., 213-744-7400, www.casciencectr.org), formerly known as the California Museum of Science and Industry, where you can get down with modern science and technology via hands-on exhibits that teach the kids about the environment, aerospace, math, energy, health, and economics. And if that isn't enough, mosey on over to the **California African-American Museum**

(600 State Dr., Exposition Park, 213-892-1333, www.caam.ca.gov). Rotating exhibits highlight the African-American experience through photographs, artifacts, oral histories, and videos. Just reopened after a $3 million dollar renovation in September of 2002. Call for info. Nearby you've also got the **Natural History Museum of Los Angeles County** (www.nhm.org), 900 Exposition Blvd., 213-763-DINO. Dinosaur fossils, tropical rainforests, and more. Open 9:30a.m.-5p.m. Monday-Friday, Saturday and Sunday 10 a.m.-5 p.m. Admission: $8 adults, $5.50 for students 12-17 and seniors (62+), $2 children 5-12, free for children under 5. Free the first Tuesday of each month.

In its newly renovated building, the **Japanese-American Museum** (www.janm.org, 369 E. First St., 213-625-0414) is a former Buddhist temple built in 1925. The museum is the first in this country devoted to the history and contributions of Japanese-Americans. Originally opened in '92, the new museum opened its doors to the public in January of '99 with 30,000 more square feet of exhibit space. The strikingly beautiful curving glass building was designed by Gyo Obata, who also designed the Smithsonian Air and Space Museum in Washington DC. Tuesday-Sunday 10a.m.-5p.m., Thursday 10a.m.-8p.m. Closed Mondays, Thanksgiving Day, Christmas Day, and New Year's Day. Free every Thursday from 5-8p.m. and every third Thursday of the month. Adults $6, seniors $5, students with ID and children 6-17 $3. Children under 5 and museum members, free. Special group rates and rentals available.

One of the most spectacular places worth visiting in the Los Angeles area is the **Huntington Library and Botanical Gardens** (www.huntington.org, 1151 Oxford Rd, San Marino, 626-405-2100). Located within the small exclusive area known as San Marino, adjacent to the city of Pasadena, this oasis of art and culture is set on 150 magical acres of gardens. Older kids will be enchanted but more astute younger ones may enjoy this as well. Guaranteed that appreciative adults will be in awe. In addition to the Rose Garden, Japanese Tea Garden (where you can purchase snacks for the colorful giant koi fish, the kids will love this), Bonsai Garden, Zen Garden, Desert Garden, Shakespeare Garden, Herb Garden, Cactus Garden, and more gardens galore, the grounds also are home to three art galleries (come see Gainsborough's masterpiece *The Blue Boy*). A truly magnificent library housing a rare books and manuscripts collection features rotating exhibits. The food in the restaurant is actually a cut above most museum fare and not too pricey. English tea served in the Rose Garden daily except Mondays, reservations recommended. Open Tuesday-Friday: Noon to 4:30 p.m. Saturday and Sunday: 10:30 a.m.-4:30 p.m. Closed Mondays and major holidays. Members: Free. Non-members: $10 adults, $8.50 seniors age 65 and over, $7 students age 12 and older, and free for children under 12. Group rates are $8 for groups of ten or more. And here is one of the best deals in all of LA; admission is free on the first Thursday of every month! Don't miss this one! It is something that you and your kids will long remember and will want to visit time and again. Sorry, no picnics or pets.

The **Los Angeles County Museum of Art** (www.lacma.org, 5905 Wilshire Blvd. two blocks east of Fairfax, 323-857-6000), housing one of the world's largest art collections, is a hot spot of activity. Pre-Columbian to the hip modern. Also a great place for film, live music and poetry readings; check the listings. Free jazz Friday nights during the spring and summer months in the promenade. Open Monday, Tuesday and Thursday 11:30 a.m.-8p.m., Friday 11:30 a.m.-9 p.m., Saturday and Sunday 11 a.m.-8 p.m. Closed Wednesdays, Thanksgiving and Christmas. Admission: $7 adults, $5 for students 18+ and seniors 62+, $1 young children, free for children under 5. Free second Tuesday of every month. Located next door to the world famous **La Brea Tar Pits** (5801 Wilshire Blvd., 323-934-7243) where the sticky black tar still bubbles and burps, and the **George C. Page Museum** where you can see all those sabertooth tiger and dinosaur bones that are still being retrieved from the active pits. Open Tuesday-Sunday 10 a.m.-5 p.m. Adults $6, seniors 62+ and students with ID $3.50, children 5-10 $2. Members and children under 5 free.

If you dig car culture like I do (proud owner of two vintage Caddy's and a '65 Riviera), the **Petersen Automotive Museum** (6060 Wilshire Blvd. in the Miracle Mile District. 323-930-2277, www.petersen.org) is an absolute must see! Zoom on down. If you have family members that are into vintage American steel, and especially teenagers with learner's permit in hand who can't wait to rule the road, then don't hesitate, this place will blow your mind. A gearhead's wet dream come true. Floors of vintage cars – race cars, show cars, funny cars, hot rods, and low riders… you name it. Also an entire floor of vintage motorcycles! Get yer motors runnin'… head out on the highway… Open Tuesday-Sunday, 10a.m. - 6p.m. Adults $7, children 5-12 $5, seniors $6, members and children under 5 free.

In the heart of downtown LA, directly across the street from **Union Station** (take the time to walk across the street and see this incredible deco structure, often a location in many films), rests the historic and very active **Olvera Street** (www.olvera-street.com) which rests inside **El Pueblo De Los Angeles Public Park** at 845 N. Alameda St., the founding site of our dear City of Angels. Open everyday from 10 a.m.-7 p.m., this Mexican marketplace is alive with many festive restaurants, shops, dancing, bolero musicians and mariachis. Several historic buildings can be found on this street including the Avila Adobe (c.1818), the Pelanconi House, which is the oldest brick house in LA (1855), and the Sepulveda House built in 1887. Get all your Mexican kitsch north of the border, including fabulous velvet paintings! If you happen to be in LA during the first week of May, come to **Cinco de Mayo** (May 5th for those not familiar with Spanish) and party large with the local folk. Cerveza, por favor!

If you would like to have lunch at one of the greatest and longest established eateries in Los Angeles, then head on over to **Phillippe's** (1001 Alameda, 213-628-3781) for their not to be beaten French dip sandwich ($4.45). Serving Angelenos since 1908, it has sawdust on the floors and history on the walls, and you are guaranteed to experience downtown and Los Angeles at its most diverse through the regular clientele that have made this place a tradition for almost a century. The food is great, and the mustard is hot! Open 6 a.m.-10 p.m. everyday.

While downtown, stop in at **Bob Baker's Marionette Theater** (1345 W. 1st St., 213-250-9995) operating in the same location for almost 40 years, making it one of the longest running theaters of its kind in the entire United States. This is an incredibly unique and wonderful experience for younger children. Owned and operated by 78-year-old Bob himself, a puppeteer since the age of 8(!), Bob builds the puppets and Ursula Hienle creates the costumes. Shows are Tuesday-Friday at 10:30 a.m., Saturday and Sunday at 2:30 p.m. They do birthdays where your child is given a gift and then crowned king or queen for the day. Admission is still only $10, which includes coffee, juice or ice cream! Kids under 2 are free. Yeah, Daddy! Reservations are required. Across the street is one of the biggest open graffiti pits in all of LA. An edgy neighborhood at night, you can feel safe during the day.

Hop into your car and head west to the place that is the best at the far western end of the mother road Route 66, where you can get your kicks at **Pacific Park** (www.pacpark.com,

310-260-874) on the **Santa Monica Pier** (310-458-8900, www.santamonicapier.org). On the renovated pier, experience an all-new, full-blown, bonafide amusement park with rollercoasters, shops, food, games, and the world famous Santa Monica beachfront as a complete throwback to days gone by. Get cotton candy, corn dogs and a Coke, and then hit the surf. Plenty of places to shop, and arcades for the kids as well. Where Colorado Ave. empties into the Pacific at land's end. Park in the lot and save yourself the hassle of trying to find parking on the street above. If you come in the summer months, there are jam-packed free concerts on the pier. Check local listings or call the pier for info.

A great bookstore featuring live readings of children's lit is **Children's Bookworld** (10580 W. Pico Blvd., West LA, 310-559-2665). Three storytellers trade off on Saturdays starting at 10:30 a.m. using different storytelling techniques including puppets. Free. Up the street is the **Imagination Station** (1130 Lincoln Blvd., Santa Monica, 310-854-4196) showcasing adults telling slightly twisted fairy tales for children.

Completed in1926, architect Bertram Goodhue's Byzantine landmark **Los Angeles Central Library** is still here (www.lapl.org/central/clhp.html, 630 W. 5th St., 213-228-7000). Having survived two arson attacks in April and September of 1986, the library was finally reopened to an eager public in 1993 after a complete and modern renovation and restoration. The library has many activities for children and families, including storytelling, plays and musical events. The interior display alone is well worth the visit – the 1928 California history murals, friezes, varied statuary, vast modern atrium, reading rooms and the new theatrical facilities provide a fascinating study of the old and new in both art and design. The Central Library is situated in the real heart of downtown Los Angeles resting in the shadow of the **Library Tower** at 633 W.

5th St., the single tallest structure west of the mighty Mississippi. The wonderful and diverse Jud Fine art plan at the **Maguire Gardens** outside the library are an urban oasis where you can picnic, relax and read a good book. Call for schedules and events.

Beyond cliché pizza-joints-with-arcades, there lies under the umbrella of the Beverly Hills zip code a rowdy, loud and obnoxious, interactive eatery known as **Ed Debevic's** (134 N. La Cienega, 310-659-1952) where they boast that there is nothing on the menu over $9. A totally retro place done in '50s chrome and vinyl, the waiters and waitresses are all in character and costume running the gamut of '50s, '60s and '70s pop culture. They sing, they dance, they joke, they scream, they work for their tips. While it is true that most of the waiters and waitresses in LA either are or want to be in "the business", the hired help here are *allowed* to be and probably are. The place can be tons of fun for everyone in the tribe and the food is actually not too bad. Good shakes. Come for the fun! They do birthdays. The hours vary in January through the first week of March, so call ahead.

Last, but certainly not least, get yourselves down to the place where the locals go for toys, gadgets, movie kitsch, fake blood, magic paraphernalia, costumes, and loads more fun stuff you will never need at **Hollywood Toys & Costume** (6600 Hollywood Blvd., 323-464-4444) Located in sick and twisted touristy Hollywood on the Walk of Fame, among the funky wig shops (where you can have a shocking blue Godzilla-sized Elvis pompadour made to order in just about an hour for around $70), head shops, poster stores, and nasty clothing boutiques, this place is really pretty special. Go there just to look if nothing else. It's a wonderland of toys and gadgets for the kids, and lots of fun stuff for the parents too. Everything from monster masks and Barbies to collectible horror flick models that can set ya back a couple of C-notes; this is real live Hollywood, baby!

Well, there ya go, boys and girls. Just a few places for Mom, Dad, and the kiddies to enjoy that basically won't break the bank. So get on board, have fun, and be safe. Don't leave your kids or the pets in the car alone, bring your Ray Bans, sunscreen in the summer, and lots of quarters for the meters year round, 'cause the parking Gestapo is fast and furious here in lovely LA. It's rare that you will get a ticket for speeding as long as ya go with the flow, and I would strongly recommend that you stay off all freeways during rush hours (6:30-9 a.m., 3:30-7 p.m). May the wind be at your back and the road rise up to meet you; or as they say in sunny Southern California: Have a nice day, dude! Let's do lunch. Have my people call your people. Love ya! No *really*, love ya…

ART-I-FACTS
nancy Whalen

The underground art scene in Los Angeles is something to be proud of. It is a dynamic and inspiring reflection of our diverse city. Despite a lack of public funding and increased governmental interest in censorship, the underground art scene in Los Angeles is growing, thriving, and supporting itself financially. Many new artistic communities have evolved and galleries have sprung up in various pockets of the city, like Highland Park and Chinatown. In well-established "artistic" communities such as Echo Park, many new galleries have opened in the past few years in storefronts and houses. Almost all of LA's artistic communities and groups of galleries support each other by having gala openings on the same nights.

This chapter will be useful both for emerging artists looking for new spaces to show, as well as for collectors and those seeking something interesting, "cutting edge" or irreverent.

La Luz de Jesus/Wacko, (4633 Hollywood Boulevard, Los Feliz, 323-663-0122, Hours: 11am-7pm Mon-Sat, Sun Noon-6pm, www.laluzdejesus.com) La Luz de Jesus has a long and colorful history. Its adjoining store Wacko started as the Soap Plant in 1971 in Silver Lake, then moved to Melrose Avenue pioneering the early artiness of that once quiet and now world-famous area. It was on Melrose that the La Luz de Jesus Gallery was started and held regular art openings for years cultivating a huge underground following. Currently Wacko and La Luz reside in Los Feliz, where the gallery features contemporary artists, both established and emerging. It specializes in art that is sometimes referred to as "No Brow"; a term coined by Robert Williams signifying anti-establishment work that is the opposite of highbrow art. The gallery specializes in illustrators, comic strip artists, and animators. La Luz has openings the first Friday of every month. One major group show is held every year to introduce new artists; throughout the year they have two and four person shows. If you are interested in showing, please send slides or samples of work and information about yourself with a self-addressed stamped envelope. They take a long time to review work, but do get back to people.

On the corner of Sunset and Alvarado between the neighborhoods of Silver Lake and Echo Park is a new art colony which is socialistic and idealistic. This communal haven currently consists of an art collective space, a café, and a film center. Coming soon is a magazine shop and a public library.

Labor Fruit (1200 North Alvarado St., LA, 213-413-5550, www.laborfruit.com) Nurturing a wave of local designers while sucking sales from the cold clutches of corporate clothing is one of Labor Fruit's mottos. It's a cosmopolitan boutique crossed with a bohemian craft movement. Anything that anyone makes or designs that's functional and one–of-a-kind will be considered for showing. Everyone who works there (many donate their time) does what he or she can to make the space successful. Labor Fruit provides artisans a place to profit from their work, which they feel helps artists to further develop and articulate their craft. If you want to show at Labor Fruit, bring your work in. Handcrafted books, pen, lanterns with jewels, hand-beaded scarves, ceramics, t-shirts, photography, and candles are a few things on display.

Echo Park Film Center (1200 North Alvarado St, LA, www.polyesterprince.com) Owned by an Italian social art activist, the Echo Park Film Center is dedicated to keeping the cinematic revolution alive. "Sell your TV and come to the cinema" is one of their slogans. The mission is to empower everyday people to make films by selling filmmaking (primarily super-8) equipment at the lowest prices in town, repairing old equipment at reasonable prices, making equipment available on a complimentary basis, and giving classes. Local art hangs on the walls and routinely changes. Thursday nights at 8 pm the center screens underground films and pays the filmmakers (who often speak before the screenings) with the $5 door donations. Some recent screenings included home videos projected on the building's side for the traffic driving by, a film called "The Subconscious Art of Graffiti Removal," and a human rights film festival.

An oasis of art galleries can be found on the 1500 Block of Echo Park Boulevard in Echo Park. Started four years ago by the opening of the Ojala' gallery, several other galleries opened in its wake turning abandoned storefronts into the centerpiece of the Echo Park art community. For current news, www.echopark.net has listings of what's going on in the galleries and art community in this area. Generally the galleries on this block have openings once a month on the same night and make it a big party.

TO LOS ANGELES

Ojala' (1547 Echo Park Ave., LA, 213-250-4155, www.echoparkarts.org) Ojala' was the first gallery on the block. Owner/curator Jesus Sanches lives in Echo Park, has many friends who are artists, and was surprised there were no galleries in the neighborhood, so he opened one. Ojala' shows only artists who live or work in the Echo Park area. The small café in the back of the gallery serves a mean cappuccino. If you are interested in showing, drop off slides or images. They usually do one-man shows due to the small size of the gallery, and the wait time for a show is up to one year.

Fototeka (1549 Echo Park Ave, LA, 213-250-4686, fototeka@yahoo.com) This space specializes in affordable photography created by emerging local and international artists. It is owned by a husband and wife team who help artists organize their work and hang their shows since many artists are first-timers. If you are interested in showing here, send a bio and slides.

Nicole Dintaman Gallery (1555 Echo Park Blvd, LA, 213-977-8839, dintamangallery@earthlink.net) Nicole shows photography by emerging artists, many who haven't shown before. She likes art that incorporates new processes, and processes that haven't been accepted yet. She finds the Echo Park community incredibly supportive and most of the people buying art here are from the neighborhood. For consideration of your work, send slides or color scans, a statement and/or resume.

Delirium Tremens (1553 Echo Park Blvd, LA, 213-861-6802, Sat & Sun 1-5 pm) This innovative, fun gallery specializes in emerging artists, and has shown everything from hand-made piñatas to paintings to Lisa Mraz's baby clothing embroidered with offensive jokes.

Book Bound (1545 Echo Park Ave, LA, 213-481-0802) This tiny bookstore and art gallery is sandwiched between several other galleries on Echo Park Boulevard. You can peruse and buy zines, vintage and contemporary books, and they have very cheap paperbacks and chapbooks as well. The space features local art on the walls, (a lot of it created by musicians), and holds weekly readings by local and touring writers. Artists are welcome to bring in art to be considered for showing.

Show Pony (1543 Echo Park Blvd, LA) This space is half art gallery and half clothing boutique. There are new shows every month with themes such as 'science fair' or 'Burning Man.' Kimmy, the owner/curator, is open to artists bringing in their work in person.

The old part of Chinatown is exotic, culturally rich and has reasonable rents. The art scene flourishes here among the herb doctors, rice paper umbrellas, and chow mein. Most of the galleries are located along a quiet, closed-off boulevard called Chung King Road. Many of the galleries have moved into old Chinese storefronts and kept the original signage out front, naming their space after what the old stores were called, like Black Dragon. The galleries have openings every five weeks, usually on Saturday nights. There is a nice sense of community here.

Dianne Pruess Gallery, (945 Chung King Rd, LA, 213-687-8226, diannepruess@hotmail.com) This gallery, which used to be a vase store, specializes in thoughtful work from East Africa, according to curator Joel Mesler. He says that he met the owner of the gallery while in jail on charges that he'd rather not elaborate on. For consideration, bring in or send in work.

China Art Objects, 933 Chung King Rd, LA, 213-613-0384) This gallery has the distinction of having been the first to open on Chung King Road about three years ago. It shows work in all mediums.

INMO Gallery (971 Chung King Rd, LA, 213-626-4225,

www.inmogallery.com) This big, beautiful, high-ceilinged space shows art that explores architectural themes and special relations. They show all mediums from emerging and established artists. For consideration, send in slides, bio, and mission statement.

Acuna-Hansen Gallery (427 Bernard St, LA, 323-441-1624, conart@aol.com) This gallery specializes in unique art from emerging artists. Just off Chung King Road, openings occur on the same nights.

Highland Park, home to many talented Latino artists, finally has some galleries reflecting this neighborhood's personality and cultural flavor. Highland Park is the latest artistic community to form a cluster of galleries, primarily along Figueroa Street.

Galleria Mundo, (4022 N. Figueroa St, LA, 323-227-9127. 11am – 7pm Wed – Sat. By appointment Mondays & Tuesdays.) This gallery is owned by an amazing female painter who shows all mediums in both group and one-man shows.

Rock Rose, (4108 N. Figueroa, Highland Park, 323-222-4740, Mon-Fri 5pm-10pm; Sat 12pm–4pm) Rock Rose is an art gallery, coffeehouse, and bookstore. They also host live shows of spoken word, performance art, and music, and offer art and theater classes for children.

Gallery Figueroa (6122 North Figueroa St., Highland Park, 323-258-5939, www.galleryfigueroa.com) Performance art space showing vibrant, brave pieces on all subjects.

Rachel Rosenthal Performance Art Theater & Workshop Space (2847 South Robertson Blvd, LA, 310-839-0661, www.rachelrosenthal.com) Rachel Rosenthal is one of the pioneers of performance art, which she has participated in and strongly influenced since the 1950s. She founded this space more than 20 years ago and has been producing, teaching, and staging the most innovative and profound performance art ever.

This space presents eight-week workshops on a seasonal basis. The high-caliber company, which performs periodically, is well worth seeing at least a couple of times.

Highways (1651 18th St, Santa Monica, 310-453-1755. www.highwaysperformance.org) Highways is one of Southern California's boldest centers for new performance. Highway's mission is to develop and present innovative performance and visual art among people of diverse cultural identities and foster a critical dialogue among artists concerning social issues and the communities they serve. Highways features theatrical, dance, comedy and dramatic shows, festivals, gallery exhibitions, and community rituals. They also provide training in performance, writing and movement.

California Institute of Abnormal Arts, aka C.I.A. (11334 Burbank Blvd., Burbank, 818-506-6353) Owned by Carl Crew, this is a place where the more "out there" a performer is, the better. Wednesday, Friday, and Saturday nights feature live music and performances of various types.

Los Angeles Contemporary Exhibits (6522 Hollywood Blvd., LA, 323-957-1777, www.artleak.org, Wed–Sat noon to 6pm) This space shows all media formats. It is more than a gallery because this organization assists artists in producing shows. They assist in writing grant proposals or obtaining funds, or the staff might help in the creation of the work in collaboration with artists. If you are interested in having a show, submit a mission statement and biography of the project you have in mind.

LITERARY LOS ANGELES
David L. Ulin

For the last few years, one of my favorite stories about Los Angeles has been the one that says the city is now the number one book-buying market in the country. That's right, not New York, not Boston or Chicago or San Francisco, but Los Angeles — the American city where the most books are bought and sold. Of course, such a statistic only tells us *how much*, not *what*, people bring home from the bookstore ("fifty million copies of *Dianetics*," one jaded friend muttered when I asked what she thought), but at least it suggests that *something* is going on. For decades, after all, LA has been written off as an illiterate culture, in which reading fades along with brain cells beneath the beat of the relentless sun. There are no books or readers in Los Angeles, or so conventional wisdom dictates;

if you're a writer here, you must write for Hollywood. And Hollywood, well... as Raymond Chandler sneered in 1945, "(The) very nicest thing Hollywood can possibly think of to say to a writer is that he is too good to be only a writer."

The irony is that, for all its new-found status as a book-buying center, Los Angeles is not a great bookstore city, and probably hasn't been since Chandler's era, when Hollywood Boulevard was lined with bookshops, and even a tough guy like Philip Marlowe might wander into one, as he does in *The Big Sleep*, to get information on a case. By now, most of the bookstores have long since scattered, leaving in their wake a city where bookselling is, for the most part, as generic as the endless sprawl of shopping centers and tract houses, an environment dominated by superstores. To be fair, I *have* found some good stuff in those places; not long ago, I scored an obscure small press haiku collaboration by Jack Kerouac at the **Brentano's** in the Beverly Center (8500 Beverly Blvd, West Hollywood; 310-652-8024). But at their core, chains are anti-literary, staffed by people who don't know much more than last month's bestsellers, and stocked almost exclusively with mainstream titles, which makes the experience of browsing in one about as stimulating as shopping at the Gap.

If you're looking for a different kind of bookstore experience, LA still has a handful of good independents, the kind of places that give a print freak like myself a bit of hope. My favorite is **Book Soup** (8818 Sunset Blvd, West Hollywood; 310-659-3110), across the street from Tower Records at the eastern edge of the Sunset Strip. With a knowledgeable staff, wide selection, and the willingness to order books from anywhere in the world, Book Soup is not only the best bookstore in Los Angeles, it's one of the best bookstores I've ever been in, comfortable, cozy, smelling of print and paper, a floor-to-ceiling-lined rabbit warren of shelves where you can lose yourself for hours. Although it specializes in art books, Book Soup also features a comprehensive selection of literature and fiction, and next door, at the aptly named **Book Soup Addendum**, you can buy remainders and publishers overstock titles at discount prices. There's also a newsstand in the alley leading to the parking lot, which stocks a vast array of literary journals, foreign newspapers, and magazines.

Perhaps the only other LA bookstores as all-encompassing as Book Soup are **Dutton's Brentwood Bookstore** (11975 San Vicente Blvd, Brentwood; 310-476-6263) and **Vroman's Bookstore** (695 East Colorado Blvd, Pasadena; 626-449-5320), both of which call themselves community bookshops, relying on one-to-one relationships with readers and writers to serve a particular clientele and neighborhood. Dutton's is a small complex of storefronts arranged around a central courtyard, more a collection of shops (each with its own theme, from children's literature to gift books) than one unified bookstore; Vroman's, on the other hand, has been a Pasadena institution for 108 years. Yet other, smaller bookstores have adapted the community model also, from **Esowon Books** (3655 South La Brea Ave, LA; 323-294-0324), which specializes in African-American literature and authors to **Children's Book World** (10580 3/4 West Pico Blvd, West Los Angeles; 310-559-2665), an especially marvelous oasis in the commercial wasteland of West LA, with more than four thousand children's books that jump out from the shelves like three-dimensional reminders of why we all started reading in the first place. Then there's **Skylight Books** (1818 Vermont Ave, Los Feliz; 323-660-1175), a relatively new bookstore that focuses on LA literature; it opened in 1996, in the space vacated when another independent, Chatterton's, closed.

The Skylight story makes for a rare bit of reclamation in the independents' struggle for survival; its very existence is a moral victory against the chains. The same is true in a different way of **Midnight Special Bookstore** (1318 Third Street Promenade, Santa Monica; 310-393-2923), which, since the early 1990s, has remained afloat despite having lost forty percent of its business to Borders and Barnes & Noble, which effectively surround it on Santa Monica's Third Street Promenade. Midnight Special is an LA institution, a store that opened in 1970 as a political collective, and still retains its leftist edge. On its shelves, you'll find material from literature to obscure Marxist rags and volumes of anarchist theory, and in the back of the store, a "cultural center" showcases readings and lectures on a similar set of subjects and themes.

Of course, when to comes to readings, Midnight Special is just one of many venues in Los Angeles; this is the home of stand-up poetry, after all. Perhaps the best-known place to catch a reading is **Beyond Baroque** (681 Venice Blvd, Venice; 310-822-3006), which, since 1968, has provided a home for author appearances, writing workshops, and small press publications that might not otherwise see the light of day. If not for Beyond Baroque, in fact, there would be no literary Los Angeles; literally dozens of the city's most iconic poets and writers got started there. Over the last decade, however, Beyond Baroque has gone through some rough times; it almost failed in the mid-1990s, and has never quite recovered its position of eminence on the literary scene. These days, the place is solvent, and its ramshackle barn of a building (the former Venice City Hall) is cleaner and better staffed than it's been in years. But when it comes to programming, Beyond Baroque's just not as adventurous as it once was, and it's been a long time since it's broken any real new ground.

For a truly vibrant reading space, try the **UCLA Hammer Museum** (10899 Wilshire Blvd, Westwood; 310-443-7000), which hosts a number of different reading series, from Contemporary American Poetry to Urban Poetry/Spoken Word. My own favorite (and not just because I've read in it) is the New American Writing series curated by Benjamin Weissman, who for many years ran the Friday night readings at Beyond Baroque. New American Writing features not just local but national talent, and is centered by Weissman's iconoclastic personality and wit. One Halloween, for instance, during a group reading of ghost stories, he did the introductions wearing a set of fake breasts and a weightlifter's outfit, and insisted everyone read in costume. This doesn't mean Weissman doesn't take literature seriously; he does. But he also wants to have fun with it, to remind us that readings should be entertaining, a message that can get lost in literary culture, where accessibility often takes a back seat to angst.

The Hammer Museum is not alone among museums and galleries in hosting literary readings; since 1994, the **Los Angeles County Museum of Art** (5905 Wilshire Boulevard; 323-857-6000) has featured the Writers in Focus series, directed by poet Laurel Ann Bogen, where poets perform in front of paintings, while **Bergamot Station/Track 16 Gallery** (2525 Michigan Avenue, C1, Santa Monica; 310-264-4678), a converted commuter rail station, sponsors a wide cross-section of readings and discussions by writers and theorists in a gallery setting, offering a multi-dimensional way of experiencing literary (and other) art. The peripatetic **Writers Bloc** (310-655-8587), meanwhile, changes its setting with every event, staging readings in museums, theatres, and even synagogues, and attracting a formidable field of big-name talent, from Joan Didion and Kurt Vonnegut to Elmore Leonard and Richard Ford.

It could be said that only in Los Angeles would literature end up playing itself out in public — become, in other words, a form of theater, rather than a matter for the printed page. In the end, though, that may be as it should be, for LA has never been a traditional city, nor had a traditional literary life. Here, writing is where you find it, whether in the densely packed shelves of your local bookstore, or before a painting in some airy, well-lit gallery. And when it comes to all those books that Angelenos are buying... well, to steal a line from Elvis, fifty million readers can't be wrong.

MORE LOCAL LIT BITS & POETRY READINGS

Visit the grave of LA lit legend **Charles Bukowski**, at Green Hills Cemetary, San Pedro. His eternal address is plot 875 in the Ocean View section.

Tia Chucha's Café Cultural (12737 Glenoaks Blvd., Sylmar, 818-362-7060) Author/publisher Luis J. Rodriguez now runs this happening space, with weekly open readings.

Poetry Slams (www.poetryslam.com) happen all over town—there are at least 5 different local slams.

Cobalt Café (22047 Sherman Way, Canoga Park, 818-348-3789) Lively all-ages venue has open readings on Tuesday.

Lydia Lunch hosts The Un-Happy Hour, a Sunday evening series at **The Parlour** (7702 Santa Monica Blvd., West Hollywood, 323-650-7968).

Harmony Gallery (5911-1/2 Franklin at Bronson, Hollywood, 323-957-7965) This small happening space hosts frequent readings, call for info.

World Stage (4344 Degnan Blvd., Leimert Park Village, LA, 323-293-2451) hosts open readings and writing workshops... sometimes all in the same night! Call for schedule.

Nile River Coffeehouse (5819 W. Pico Blvd., LA, 323-525-0315) Sunday evenings: "Nights Over Egypt" poetry series.

Beyond Baroque (681 Venice Blvd., Venice, 310-822-3006) is a hotbed of non-stop action for literati types. Call or check local papers for readings and workshops schedule.

THE RECORD WEASEL'S GUIDE
Dan Epstein

Every time I pass a record store, I feel like an alcoholic passing a bar. Regardless of my prior obligations, time restrictions, or utter lack of cash, I feel the overwhelming, all-consuming NEED to go in and rifle through the bins. Consequently, I've spent more time in LA record stores than most local actors spend at outdoor cafés. But weep not for my affliction, dear readers; rather, rejoice that I have wasted my time so that you don't have to. Whether you're jonesing for a clean vinyl copy of the first Funkadelic LP, buying a copy of Sheryl Crow's latest meisterwerk "for a friend," or just trying to get rid of a trunkload of shitty promos, the following should help you score with a minimum amount of hassle and inconvenience.

THE UNDERGROUND GUIDE

Amoeba Music (6400 Sunset Blvd., Hollywood, 323-245-6400) The buzz about the Hollywood arrival of this Bay Area mainstay was so intense, record weasels from all over Southern California began lining up outside the night before its opening in November 2001. While I skipped the Day One feeding frenzy (hey, I'm not THAT much of a loser!), I did sashay over a few days afterwards and found the hype to be completely justified. Simply put, Amoeba is the BIGGEST FUCKING RECORD STORE I'VE EVER SEEN, with an inventory that includes everything from ancient blues 78s to Italian horror flick DVDs to vintage psychedelic concert posters. The prices are good, the selection is astounding, and — best of all — they have a friendly and knowledgeable staff that's more than happy to help you navigate the endless aisles of goodies. The store also has separate checkout and trade-in counters, which means that you don't have to wait around forever to have a buyer appraise the items you're looking to unload. A word of warning, however: it's best to approach Amoeba with a list of things you're looking for; more than a few innocent browsers have wound up lost and disoriented, and in some cases have gone missing for days.

Aaron's (1150 N. Highland Ave., Hollywood, 323-469-4700) Once the hippest, most comprehensive record store in town (or at least for those who avoid the Westside like the plague), Aaron's star has dimmed considerably. They still have a pretty decent selection of '50s R&B, Latin jazz, '60s garage, '70s Reggae, show tunes, and alternative rock, as well as many rows of used CDs, used vinyl, and a whole bunch of previously-viewed videos and DVDs. Not to mention that Aaron's is still the only store in the city with a comprehensive Prog section. But with the recent arrival of the nearby Amoeba Music, Aaron's is starting to look pretty crummy by comparison. Of course, the store hasn't exactly risen to the challenge from its upstart neighbor — the rock/imports/oldies section (yes, they just mash 'em all together) is still bafflingly (dis)organized, the tiny parking lot is still the sort of thing Ed Wood might describe as a "nightmare of horror," and the staff remains defiantly unhelpful. In other words, why bother with Aaron's when the far-superior Amoeba is only a mile away?

Atomic Records (3812 W. Magnolia Blvd., Burbank, 818-848-7090) The best Burbank/Glendale store by a long shot, Atomic delivers da goods, especially if you're looking for stuff in the Exotica vein. Lotsa vinyl, CDs, and videos, the staff is laid-back and knowledgeable, and they claim to pay "the best" prices for used shit. Their own prices aren't always great — their Yellow Pages ad promises "collectable records," and you know what THAT means — but you can turn up some cheap treasures with a bit of digging.

Benway Records (1600 Pacific Ave., Venice, 310-396-8898) Inside this psychedelic shack lurks masses of vinyl, trashy videos, great new and used CDs, plus a staff that's full of fun facts, sleazy gossip and helpful hints. Las Vegas transplants Ron and Kelly Benway run this store and a branch in Vegas. (Chat them up, bring them gifts: they are two of the funniest, nicest people on earth - Ed.) They also own a fully-equipped lavender and shocking orange ice cream truck that occasionally visits punk rock gigs, and sells not only Sparkle Bars and Eskimo Pies, but also a full line of punk CDs, vinyl, and t-shirts.

Eastside Records (1813 Hillhurst Ave., Los Feliz, 323-913-7461) Blink and you'll miss it; this odd little used CD and vinyl store is located in one of Los Feliz's more unassuming strip malls. The Rock and Jazz bins are disconcertingly half-empty at best (though they do have more copies of Foreigner's *Head Games* LP than I've ever seen in one place). The place evidently does a brisk trade in used Classical vinyl. The cheaply priced CDs are pretty much worthless (unless, of course, you've been looking everywhere for that elusive copy of Mandy Patinkin's *Dress Casual*), but you will occasionally find some gems among the junk.

Heavy Rotation (12354 Ventura Blvd., Studio City, 818-769-8882) Nestled on a bustling stretch of Ventura Blvd., Heavy Rotation is just a convenient hop, skip and jump away from Hollywood. Not coincidentally, this place has become a favorite dumping ground for record company employees to sell off extra promo copies of their label's latest releases, which in turn results in an extensive selection of "used" new titles (the selection of sealed product pales by comparison). No imports, but the prices are extremely reasonable, and there always seems to be a sale on used vinyl (one lucky day, I scored all five Nick Gilder LPs for under five bucks, total). There are also plenty of used video games, as well as a video bin full of such previously viewed bargains as *Lingerie Workout 2* and *Mutilator VIII*. Insider tip: the friendly owner, Pete, will usually give you a better trade-in deal if you tell him a raunchy joke!

Melrose Music (7714 Melrose Ave., 323-782-9320) A welcoming little hole-in-the wall around the corner from Fairfax High, Melrose Music specializes in the latest punk and hardcore records, but also has a surprisingly good selection of psychedelic, garage and soul reissues. There's an intriguing selection of classic punk 45s, as well as a nice array of unusual rock t-shirts. Approach with caution on weekend mornings, however; Ed, the pomadoured proprietor, has been know to enjoy before-noon spins of Nick Cave's "The Weeping Song" at deafening volume.

Moby Disc (2114 Wilshire Blvd., Santa Monica, 310-828-2887) Yer basic new'n'used outlet with import singles, intelligent stock selection, and a friendly staff. Also has a special KCRW section, which makes it easy for yuppie fucks and other Westside zombies to purchase whatever is in regular rotation on their favorite public radio station.

Penny Lane (1349 Third St. Promenade, Santa Monica, 310-319-5333) It's really not worth going out of your way for, but if you're trapped for an afternoon in Santa Monica's hellish Third Street Promenade shopping district, it's a good place to kill some time. An extensive, reasonably-priced selection of used CDs and the latest music mags...

The Record Collector (7809 Melrose Ave., Hollywood, 323-655-6653) Pristine rare jazz and classical LPs for hardcore audiophiles only; but this place is definitely not for the faint of wallet. If you're looking to sell off your mint-condition Living Stereo LPs, though, by all means do it here, and not at next-door neighbor Aaron's.

Record Rover (12204 Venice Blvd., Mar Vista, 310-390-3132) If you're looking to stock your jukebox, this tiny shop has a ton of used and reissue 45s to dig through. They also sell blank jukebox tags, 45 sleeves, and many other arcane treats for the vinyl collector. Not a bad selection of used LPs and CDs, either.

Record Surplus (11609 W. Pico Blvd., West LA, 310-478-4217) A warehouse-sized venerable treasure trove of vinyl. Sure, there are a few racks of used CDs, videos, DVDs and 45s, but Record Surplus is first and foremost a shrine to the glory of the vinyl LP. Rock, Jazz, Exotica, Oldies — they've got it on vinyl by the ton, and at fairly respectable prices, too. The 92¢ bin upstairs is a great place to shop for "guilty pleasures" (I was able to complete my Billy Squier collection here) as well as a wonderful memory jogger about now-obscure acts from the '80s.

Rhino Records (1720 Westwood Blvd., 310-474-3786; also at 2028 Westwood Blvd., 310-474-8685) A popular record weasel shopping spot sine 1973, this Westwood landmark recently made like a banana and split into two locations: The old location at 1720 Westwood Blvd. has been transformed into a bargain outlet (all used CDs and vinyl priced under five clams) while the new "Super Duper Store" location at 2028 Westwood Blvd. has the great selection of imported and domestic Rock, R&B, Rockabilly, Surf, Country, Oldies, Jazz, Blues, and World Music that Rhino's long been known for. Though the store was obviously overdue for expansion, the new arrangement is a little unsettling (especially for longtime Rhino devotees) — you miss the warmth and bustle of the old space (which now seems grungy and under-populated), while the new space seems about as sterile as the Virgin Megastore.

Rockaway Records (2395 Glendale Blvd., Silverlake, 323-664-3232) A Mecca for record collectors from around the world, Silverlake's only decent record emporium boasts signed-and-framed rock posters from the past three decades, as well as all kinds of rare records. If you seek the latter, it helps to know what you're looking for; they keep them hidden in the back, and you have to go to the special "collectibles" counter to present your "want list". (On the positive side, they pay really well for hard-to-find vinyl.) The plentiful used CDs are dirt cheap (new CDs are priced nicely, as well). New rock books, dog-eared copies of *Hit Parader*, and everything readable in-between is here, and my favorite part is the "unsorted 45s" bin, where some unbelievable gems lurk among the thousands of Mr. Mister singles — once, I even found a promo copy of "Action Man," a single from the Village People's "new romantic"-oriented *Renaissance* LP.

Tower Sunset (8801 Sunset Blvd., 310-657-7300) Unquestionably the best mainstream record store in LA, Tower has long been THE place to go when you're looking for the latest hits at reasonable prices. Some people dis the joint for its snotty employees and cramped aisles, but the place is well stocked beyond belief, putting the nearby Virgin Megastore to shame at every turn.

Vinyl Fetish (7305 Melrose Ave., 323-935-1300; and 1750 N. Vermont Ave., 323-660-4500) Featuring a limited selection and an unlimited pricing policy, Vinyl Fetish's two stores are mostly a waste of time — unless you have something specific in mind, and are willing to pay through the nose for it.

Virgin Megastore (8000 Sunset Blvd., 323-650-8666) As a record store, Virgin is a pretty good place to buy movies. There's a good, fairly-priced selection of videos, laserdiscs and video games upstairs, and the store's late hours make it an ideal place to watch drunken guys trying to impress their dates by buying them the latest Madonna CD. It's a good way to kill time if you're waiting to see a movie at the adjacent Laemmle theaters.

THRIFTY LA
Nancy Whalen & Anthony Bernal

Thrift store shopping has changed drastically as its popularity has exploded: there are some high-priced pickings in places where you used to find amazing shit for a song. Now used clothing stores (privately-run thrift stores) pop up on virtually every corner. Run by entrepreneurs who mark up the goods they collect from garage sales and non-profit thrift stores, they are the people in the aisles of St. Vincent de Paul pulling fifty shirts off the rack, including the one you are about to try on. The same people who go to garage sales at 6 a.m., waking up the owner and pummeling through the junk before it's put out. Many of the larger vintage stores bid for goods donated to Salvation Army and St. Vincent de Paul before they're put out on the floor - these non-profits got smart after watching for years as truckloads of amazing stuff was bought in bulk and resold at much higher prices. This contributes to the slim pickings at some of the large non-profit thrift stores.

On the bright side, many of the owners of the used/vintage clothing stores have good taste; hence you can find great stuff in these stores without the hassle of pawing through a bunch of garbage. Also, because the market is so competitive and these stores often buy goods in bulk, sometimes you can find items for less than you'd spend at a non-profit thrift store.

Let's take a moment to talk about style. March to your own drummer, motherfucker. If you got your own style, you are immune to fluctuations of availability and prices. Continue to shop like you always have, looking as badass and breezy as ever, because you're buying stuff that you want, not necessarily what everyone else is buying. Following are the used and vintage clothing stores that have the hippest aesthetic, and the non-profit thrifts that are the biggest, the baddest, or the cheapest. All are open daily unless otherwise noted, call for hours. Bueno suerte, amigos!

VINTAGE CLOTHING STORES

Aardvarks Odd Ark (7579 Melrose. 323-655-6769) One of the first on Melrose, opening almost twenty years ago. Hawaiian and cowboy shirts, tuxedo jackets, etc. at reasonable prices. (Also, 85 Market St., Venice. 310-392-2996) Large selection of weird neckties, old silk scarves, and antique shawls; bowling shirts, gas station, mail, and truck driver uniforms; some collectible Hawaiian shirts in the $200 range, but most are $8.

Animal House (66 Windward Ave., Venice. 310-392-5411) Tasteful pretty dresses under $20, low-rider bellbottoms, Hang Ten shirts. They play chill music and have a hangout upstairs with pillows and chairs. Jim Morrison musta left his discards here.

Come To Mama (4019 Sunset at Sanborn, basement of Tsunami Cafe, Silverlake. 323-953-1275. Closed Monday.) Big groovy vibe with Nag Champa burning, old *Vogue* covers, antique kimonos, voodoo dolls, and '60s board games. The main thing here is funk, making white trash look a step up. Pimpwear, '60s Chicago ghettowear... it's all about nylon and polyester. Local bands play one Saturday every month.

Golyester (7957 Melrose, 323-655-3393. Closed Sunday.) This place has been around for years, featuring clothing, textiles, accessories, and jewelry from the 1890s to the present.

Gotta Have It (1516 Pacific, Venice. 310-392-5949) Small and packed with stuff from the last hundred years: vintage blues, jazz, and hip-hop records in the back, killer weird window displays, and very colorful dressing rooms with murals and fur on the walls.

Hidden Treasures (154 Topanga Canyon Blvd. 310-455-2998) Vintage quilts, tablecloths, etc. from the '40s and '50s; leather jackets from the '50s and '60s; they also buy vintage clothes from the public. Housed in an old health food store with a pirate on the roof, a waterfall garden, and a teepee in back.

Jet Rag (825 N. La Brea. 323-465-0128) Don't miss the Sunday parking lot sale where everything is $1! It's a big rumble fight for clothes; go early to get the good stuff. They redesign clothes, like cutting Adidas sweatpants up the middle and sewing them into a skirt. Vintage kids' clothing, and plastic bongs in assorted colors.

Junk For Joy (3314 West Magnolia Blvd., Burbank, 818-569-4903. Closed Sunday and Monday.) Specializing in dead stock: clothes from another era that have never been sold. Big selection of new '50s and '60s bathing suits, go-go boots, '70s wedding dresses.

Kathy's Boutique (11114 Magnolia Blvd., North Hollywood. 818-505-0035) I scored a Pucci jacket here: velvet with a gigantic psychedelic butterfly on the back for $29. I didn't know who Pucci was until people kept trying to buy it off my back for $500, saying they saw it in a Pucci book and that they've named their dog Pucci after him.

Ozzy Dots (4637 Hollywood Blvd., Silverlake. 323-663-2867) One of my favorite stores of all time: amazing leopard skin boots, feathered hats, sombreros, bags with peacock feathers, beautiful gowns, party dresses, ethnic clothes, '40s/'50s vintage. Almost everything is really cheap! Campy costume stuff year 'round too: bone headdresses, Star Wars torches, wigs, boas, hair glitter, gloves, stockings, false eyelashes, crazy sunglasses, fake engagement rings.

Wasteland (7428 Melrose, Hollywood. 323-653-3028) Large store with a big selection of clothes, jewelry, hats, and shoes. My favorite thing is that they'll buy your unwanted clothes or jewelry, after 1-2 hours on the waiting list, for cash or store credit.

THRIFT STORES

Boys and Girls Club of Venice (3516 Centinela at Palm, Venice. 310-391-6302) You don't belong here if you mind getting dirty and having screaming kids running around. Cheap prices, large selection of appliances, furniture, clothes and shoes, even cars and boats.

Clare Foundation Bargain Center (1002 Pico Blvd., at 10th. Closed Sunday. 310-314-6241.) This place is the way thrift stores used to be, the way they oughta be still. They believe in volume sales, their employees still remember their primary market is people without a lot of money. It feels human, not corporate and they will bargain with ya. They feature "anything we can get." We're talking hair products, radios, stoves, books, suitcases, board games, 40-cent tops, $20 couches, and a 1979 Bronco for $500.

Deseret Thrift Store (6418-1/2 Laurel Canyon, North Hollywood. Closed Sunday.) Large selections of '70s sunglasses and jewelry. Cheap and nice furniture. I got a gigantic pink sofa here for $80 that all my pals like lounging on.

Goodwill (1150 Vermont, between Sunset and Fountain; 6241 Laurel Canyon Blvd., North Hollywood. 818-980-1777) This store is reasonably priced, Ozzie Dots-adjacent, and within a few blocks of many other thrift stores. (Some other Goodwill stores: 1535 S. Western Ave., Hancock Park, 323-732-1416; 1608 Sawtelle Blvd., West Los Angeles, 310-473-9844.) If you're looking for a specific color item, it's easy to find it here since everything's lined up by color. Lots of red, purple, green, white and black, too. This is a good place for conservative work clothes (temping, anyone?), kids' clothes, men's suits for only $20, T-shirts for 99 cents, skirts for $2.99. The most expensive thing in the store is Levis for $15.99 - the other jeans are $5.99. Goodwill is a good place to go for first-look used clothes. They don't seem to be so picked over by pricing experts and private buyers. Trailers are set up in donation areas all over town and then hauled to the various stores where they unload and sell stuff a little at a time. What they can't sell goes to the clearance center store downtown. If they can't sell it there, they ship it off to Third World countries. Yikes!

Neighborhood Animal Group Thrift (Sunset Blvd., Silverlake. Closed Sunday.) Run by volunteer animal lovers, the proceeds go toward paying for animal spaying and neutering as well as hospital bills. Some items featured in this store are multicolored flowered fishing caps for $2, a small book and record section, a woven basket section, many identical glass light fixtures in a smoky gray color, $2 neckties featuring crocheted and batik designs, dummy heads with hats on them and a makeshift dressing room made out of blankets. (Next door is delicious smelling chorizo and carne asada for sale.)

Out of the Closet (12135 Victory Blvd., North Hollywood. 818-761-9777; 3160 Glendale Blvd., Atwater Village. 323-664-4394; 4136 Beverly Blvd., 213-380-8955; 4398 Sunset Blvd., Silverlake, 323-644-0525; 360 N. Fairfax Ave., 323-934-1956) There are nine Out of the Closet thrift stores benefiting AIDS-related charities. The one in North Hollywood is decorated the coolest and has the best stuff: an eclectic mix of huge old electric movie fans, '60s and '70s furniture, antique motorcycles, printing presses, old chrome fridges and washers. This store is medium cheap however - they know what they're selling.

Salvation Army (1658 11th St., at Olympic. 310-450-7235. Closed Sunday.) Large store with clothing, furniture, knicknacks.

St. Joseph's Thrift Store (404 Lincoln Blvd., Venice) They feed and clothe the homeless. Furniture and clothes for sale.

St. Matthew's (2812 Main St., Santa Monica. Closed Sundays. 310-396-9776.) Small store. Good prices. Clothing and knicknacks only.

St. Vincent de Paul's (210 N. Avenue 21, Lincoln Heights. 323-221-6191.) This place is a mainstay of hipdom. It's huge. Airplane hangar huge. The furniture is generally on the expensive side, lots of old pianos and Wurlitzers. Excellent selection of men's pants and shirts, and kids' clothes. The bargain yard in the back is the best. Though they keep changing the policy, it's something like $5 for all you can haul away and you'd be surprised how much one can haul. One time I got 500 neckties, a red metal trashcan, four art deco theater chairs, a monster truck video, and a desk. This store is most people's favorite.

YOU LOOK LIKE A MOVIE STAR, HONEY
Karen Cusolito

We know you want to look like a superstar, but first things first, meaning you'll have to start as a model. For $16 and a sense of adventure, you can be a hair model for Vidal Sassoon. So if bad hair is threatening to ruin your vacation, or if you just want to cheat on your stylist, this is the ticket.

The Beautiful People in Los Angeles pay up to $200 for a haircut, while even the Average Looking People pay around $60. What these folks don't know is you can have a Sassoon assistant cut yours for less than the cost of a parking ticket. Schedule an appointment and motor over to the **Vidal Sassoon Salon** (9403 Little Santa Monica Blvd. Beverly Hills, 310-858-9760).

An assistant, who's been through rigorous training, decides which of the 24 cuts Sassoon teaches would be good for you. This is such a well kept secret that they have to recruit people off the street to use as models. "We don't just use *anybody* as models," said Sergio, who gave me a chin-length bob. "If someone comes in with frizzed-out, waist-length hair and only wants a half-inch taken off, we won't do it." Assistants cut both men and women's hair, and do single color for $20. An instructor checks their work.

Another low-cost alternative is **Juliet Beauty Supply and Salon** (2590 Glendale Blvd. Los Angeles, 323-665-7484) in Silverlake. For $12.95, you can seat yourself in one of three chairs tucked behind rows of product and have your hair cut. Skip the "set" (aka "blow dry") which adds another $15. Single color is $30.

If it's Old Hollywood glamour you seek, try **Ball Beauty Supply** (416 N. Fairfax Ave., 323-655-2330, closed Sunday), across the street from Canter's Deli. Ball offers fascinating items like De-Lux Bob Pins with a picture of Paramount star Deborah Caulfield, Sweet Georgia Brown La La Lashes, lipstick and lip gloss, glitter body crème and a stunning assortment of false eyelashes. It's a treasure trove for drag queens and glamour pusses. After you complete your purchase (written in longhand on old-fashioned carbon-copy pads), examine your loot over a cup of chicken soup at Canter's, where the waitresses wear snoods (bought from Ball, no doubt).

For a Nuevo Hollywood look, try **Uban Natural Body** (1728 Silverlake Blvd., 323-906-0163, www.ubannaturalbody.com) which sells its own line of all-natural body products. Prices range from $8 for bath gels, to $10 for facial sprays and face wash, to $16 for a line of hemp oil products, which blend ginger and lemongrass to impart warmth and invigoration. There's also a product line dedicated to the heartbroken: Heartbreak Helper, which included "It's Not Your Fault Bath Salts," "Get a Handle Candle" and an herbal remedy to calm the emotions. The store also periodically hosts fun events like photo exhibits and psychic readings.

Next, get your nails done. There are a lot of options here; heck, there are one and a half columns of nail salons in my neighborhood phone directory! It seems $18 is the going rate for a manicure/pedicure. But check the ads in windows as you drive around town and chances are you can find it for less. **CT Nails III** (7868 Santa Monica Blvd. at Fairfax, West Hollywood, 323-656-6189) does awesome airbrushed designs for $15 a full set, or $3 a nail. At **Marinello Beauty College** (6111 Wilshire Blvd., 323-938-2005; and 716 S. Broadway, 213-627-5561; also locations in Eagle Rock, North Hollywood and Reseda, www.marinello.com), you can get a manicure/pedicure for $8.99 Maybe you wouldn't trust your hair to a beauty school pupil, but it's hard to get a bad manicure. And for that price you can afford to tip well.

Speaking of tipping (or is it tippling?), you can tip one back and get a manicure during happy hour at **Beauty Bar** (1638 N. Cahuenga Blvd., 323-464-767, open daily until 2 a.m., www.beautybar.com). If Patsy and Edina were to visit LA, this is where you'd find them. Paul Devitt has recreated a mid-'60s beauty salon in the heart of Hollywood where "beauty school dropouts" serve such reviving treatments as the "Platinum Blonde" (Stoli, rum and pineapple juice), the "Prell" and the "Shampoo". On Thursday and Friday after 6 p.m. and Saturday from 8-11 p.m., you get a manicure and a cocktail for $10. Henna tattoos are available on Friday and Saturday night.

You are now ready for a night on the town! Should you wake up a tad foggy the next morning, you might want to clear your head with a little exercise. For Angelenos, that usually means yoga. The city has tons of yoga studios and gyms that offer yoga classes. A favorite is **Ashtanga Yoga Shala** (formerly Ahimsa Yoga, 3820 Sunset Blvd. 323-660-6923, closed on Saturday and new/full moons) in a funky Silverlake storefront. Morning classes are by monthly enrollment: $135. Evening classes are $15 each or $100 for 10. Also popular is **Silverlake Yoga** (2810-1/2 Glendale Blvd. 323-953-0496). It offers five to seven classes daily, taught in the Hatha style. One class $12, six classes $65 and eight classes $80. There's also a free intro class at 2 p.m. on the first Sunday of each month.

If you're serious about yoga and are moving to the City of Angels, consider **Community Yoga** (323-661-1500, www.communityoga.org) Robert teaches out of his Silverlake area home in classes of 10 or fewer people. For that reason, you need to call him to reserve a space and get the address. But be prepared for the third degree. When a friend of mine called to tell him she would be bringing me, he wanted me to get on the line and answer a few questions. Twenty minutes later (What are your goals? What is your experience?) He gave me the go-ahead. As a dilettante, I may have failed to appreciate the instruction, but he has a devoted following nonetheless. Single classes $12, five-class pass $55, ten-class pass $100. On the first Thursday of each month, there's Yoga Sutra Study Party to "chant yoga's foundation text, enjoy a light potluck meal, and explore its relevance to everyday living." I assume he means the text, not the potluck.

Yoga not your style? There's always the good ol' YMCA. Defying the stereotypical bare-bones gymnasium dedicated to youth sports, Los Angeles has two fancy-shmancy Ys: Hollywood and Downtown LA. The **Hollywood YMCA** (1553 N. Schraeder Blvd. between Sunset and Selma, 323-467-4161, www.hollywoodwilshireymca.fitlinxx.com) is listed in the National Register of Historic Places. It underwent extensive renovation in 1995 with generous donations by such folks as

Tim Allen, who has a plaque in the courtyard. They've got all the high-tech equipment, spinning classes, and yoga you could want. You can work out for free if you're a member of another YMCA, or if you know someone who belongs, they can take you as their guest. This is where the wanna-be actors and actresses work out and while it's great for people watching, it can be depressing to realize yours is the only imperfect bod in the room.

You'll have no such insecurity at the **Ketchum Downtown YMCA** (www.ketchumdowntownymca.fitlinxx.com, 401 S. Hope St., 213-624-2348), which serves a mostly professional crowd. This is the flagship Y, designed so that the pool and exercise bikes are visible to passers-by behind glass walls. Its three-story building has the full complement of classes, exercise equipment, racquetball courts, sauna, steam room and Jacuzzi. Unlike Hollywood, the downtown Y charges $10 for other Y members.

If you'd rather skip the workout and head straight for the sauna, try **Olympic Spa** (3915 W. Olympic Blvd., 323-857-0666, www.olympicspa.citysearch.com) in Koreatown. This *women-only* spa charges $15 which includes use of the hot pool, mineral relaxation pool, jade steam sauna, dry sauna, and the "oxygen stone and bichotan charcoal therapy room." Treatments range from a $30 body scrub to a $50 Shiatsu massage to a three-hour body treatment and facial for $180.

For a non-segregated kinda clean, go to **Beverly Hot Springs** (www.beverlyhotsprings.com, 308 N. Oxford Ave., 323-734-7000). Actually, there are separate facilities for men and women. The water comes from an artesian well 2,200 feet below the surface, making it the only *natural* hot springs in the city. Admission is $40 Monday through Thursday and $50 weekends and holidays. You need an appointment for a treatment. A body scrub is $70 and a Shiatsu massage or body care conditioning is $90. Star sighting: Madonna, years ago.

Keep that healthy glow by stocking up at LA's longest-lived natural food markets: **Nowhere** (8001 Beverly Blvd., 323-658-6506) and **Erewhon** (7660 Beverly Blvd., 323-937-0777) which is Nowhere spelled backwards, sort of. Both have good selections of organic produce, natural frozen foods, juices, herbs, vitamins, homeopathic remedies, sushi and salad bars. Both are open late and a good choice for cheap meals. Eat at tables outside and soak up the scenery. Star sightings: Michael Richards at Erewhon and Jodie Foster at Nowhere restaurant (two doors down from the market).

On Sunday, hike over to **Hollywood Farmers Market** (Ivar between Sunset and Hollywood, 9 a.m. to 3 p.m.) for fresh flowers, espresso, tamales, bread, and other edible items as well as funky arts and crafts. On Saturday, the **Silverlake Farmers Market** (Sunset Blvd. at Maltman, 9 a.m. to 1 p.m.) is just getting off the ground, although whether it will survive is anyone's guess.

While you're on Sunset, it's a short drive to the corner of Virgil, where you'll find **Uncle Jer's** (4459 Sunset Blvd., 323-662-6710). It's a neighborhood landmark that's been donating a portion of its profits to humanitarian causes since before it was fashionable. Their clothes are generally ethnic, you know, those colorful garments from Ecuador and Guatemala. There's also fun stuff like plastic rings with bugs, Chinese scalp tinglers ($25), as well as an assortment of bath oils, exotic soaps and incense. Star sighting: Patricia Arquette. Next door is **Rudy's Barber Shop** (4451 W. Sunset Blvd., 323-661-6535) where guys sit on metal lawn chairs in the driveway while they wait for their $15 buzz cuts.

Down the street, where Hollywood Boulevard begins, is **Ozzy Dots** (4637 Hollywood Blvd., 323-663-2867), which has a great selection of vintage clothing, purses, hats, gloves, belts, even clown makeup. Those in the know come here to buy cheap and wacky Halloween outfits.

For real cha-cha fashion, head to **Fashions of Echo Park** (1600 W. Sunset Blvd., 213-482-1723) or **Fashion for Eva** (1557 W. Sunset Blvd., 213-250-2526). Both are open daily and stock such must-have items as 99-cent nail polish and lipstick, stick-on bras and fishnet stockings ($2.99) and animal-print underwear (three for $5).

The real Mecca for bargain hunters is the **Garment District** downtown. Skip the Cooper Building and head to **Santee Alley** (Santee St. between Maple St. and Olympic Blvd., open daily) where you'll find the cheapest knock-offs of whatever is in style at the moment including clothes, shoes, costume jewelry, makeup and kids clothing. If all that shopping works up an appetite, stop by **The Original Pantry** (877 S. Figueroa, 213-972-9279), former Mayor Richard Riordan's landmark eatery that's open 24 hours. Carnivores will enjoy the steaks and chops while vegans will shriek with horror.

PUNK LA
Shawna Kenney

LA gave birth to legendary bands like X, the Circle Jerks, the Germs, the Go-Go's, T.S.O.L., the Adolescents, Fear, etc. while SoCal in general is home to long-lived indie labels like BYO, Epitaph and Revelation Records, so of course there are still plenty of people around making good protest music. Due to the city's expansive layout it can be hard to identify any sort of unified scene in any one place — rather, punk thrives in various pockets in and around 'Hell-A.' Luckily, if you're willing to look (and drive), something's happening almost every night. Woo-hoo!

ALL AGES VENUES
"Take me to the show 'cause that's where I wanna go..." -D.I.
   Showcase Theatre (683 South Main St., Corona, 909-276-7770, booking: 909-340-0988; www.showcasetheatre.com)

Way out in the desert 'burbs of Corona about 45 minutes outside of LA proper, this club is always worth the drive. All ages hardcore, metal and punk shows every weekend with plenty of free parking and one of the best (and only) stage-dive-friendly environments in SoCal. Fuck yeah!

Chain Reaction (1652 W. Lincoln Ave., Anaheim, 714-635-6067; www.allages.com) This popular all ages venue proves there's more to Orange County than Disneyland. Catch local and national ska, indie, pop and punk bands in this low-key hangout. Fully stocked snack bar, free parking and bathrooms that always have toilet paper. Nice email 'show reminder' feature on their website, for technologically savvy punks.

The Glass House (200 West Second St., Pomona; info: 714-647-7704, box office: 909- 629-0377) Located in the Arts Colony of cute little downtown Pomona, this larger all ages venue is a great place to catch popular roc-en-español, punk and indie rock bands before they hit the Sunset Strip. Lotsa elbow room and MORE FREE PARKING!

The Smell (247 Main St., Downtown LA, 213-625-4325) It's not unusual to find hip-hop dee-jays in the front while crusty punks slam in the back of this big bombed-out warehouse that does shows the good ol' fashioned low-budget way. Cover charge is usually a "donation," benefits going on at any given time, and it's always all ages. Sketchy parking due to location — pay off a bum and your car should be safe for the night.

Cobalt Café (22047 Sherman Way, Canoga Park, 818-348-3789) All ages non-alcoholic, non-smoking venue with live music, poetry and open mic nights. Snack bar and cushy seats, too. "No slam-dancing or moshing" signs everywhere, due to some weird law in the Valley. Eat at awesome old veggie restaurant *Follow Your Heart* down the street before or after the show.

Vegan Express (3217 Cahuenga Blvd. West at Barham, LA; 323-851-8837) A punk and hippie haven for those 'in the know' – not only does this little dive make the best fake fried-chicken sandwich in the West, vegan pancakes, and killer curries, but they move the chairs outta the way and have punk shows for good causes on most Friday nights!

Headline Records (7708 Melrose Ave., LA, 323-655-2125; www.headlinerecords.com) Just like the sign says: the BEST selection and prices in Los Angeles of: New - Collector - Punk - Hardcore - Ska - Garage - Straight Edge - Grind - Import CD - Vinyl - Video - Books - T-shirts, and more! A good place to pick up cheap metal studs (the kind you wear, not date.) This truly indie store (run by scene-supportin' friendly Frenchman Jean-Luc) use to have cheap and free shows until the neighbors complained. Still hosts readings and signings by punk heroes traveling through. Excellent website and mailing list, too.

21 AND OVER VENUES
"What will you do when you turn 21…?" -the Descendents

Spaceland (1717 Silver Lake Blvd., Silverlake; info: 213-833-2843, booking: 213-662-7728) Popular with Silverlake denizens and Westside wannabes. Good place for punk, indie, art-rock and alternative shows in a comfortable setting. Great sound system. Smoking room in the back.

The Garage (4519 Santa Monica Blvd., Silverlake, 213-662-6802) 300-person capacity, okay sound depending on who's doing it. Some punk shows, but rock-n-roll and rock-a-billy rule.

Mr. T's (5621 North Figueroa St. at Ave. 57, Highland Park; hotline and Booking: 323-692-3133) You can rock, you can roll, but you can't bowl at Mr. T's bowl. You *can* see an average of 10 bands per night (and drink like a fish) for a cheap cover charge.

Whisky A Go-Go (8901 Sunset Blvd., West Hollywood, 310-652-4202) Everyone from the Doors to Janis Joplin - not to mention Blondie, the Ramones, Germs, Go-Go's, Johnny Thunders, etc - have graced the stage, and though it's still more rock than punk, the Whisky hosts many metal and hardcore acts with a sound system to die for. No stage-diving. 21 and over to drink. 18 and over to dance.

House of Blues (1530 S. Disneyland Dr., Anaheim, 714-778-BLUE) No surprises here — the latest link in the chain of H.O.B. venues is similar to its Sunset Strip counterpart, but still a good place to catch bigger Orange County bands like Social Distortion in their natural habitat.

ALSO...

Devolution Records (155 W. 2nd. St., Pomona, 909-397-41244) Punk, noise and indie vinyl, CDs, patches, badge and more, plus occasional in-store shows.

Espresso Mi Cultura (5625 Hollywood Blvd., Hollywood; 323-461-0808; bookstore: 323- 466-0481) Kick-ass coffee and tea drinks, art exhibits, author signings, and acoustic performances. Friendly Chicano/Latino-flava'd hangout — sure feels better than supportin' Starf*cks.

Café Luna Tierra Sol (2501 W. 6th St., Downtown LA; 213-380-4754, open 7 a.m. – 10 pm) Enjoy cheap organic meatless interpretations of Mexican food in this cozy co-op café (nestled in the basement of historic 1920s Asbury Apartments building.) Evening performances and readings, DJ every Monday night.

Retail Slut (7308 Melrose Ave., Hollywood; 323- 934-1339; www.retailslut.com) A fixture on Melrose since '83, this little store is THE place to get all yer punk or fetish accessories in one trip: belts, bikinis, bracelets, collars, dresses, hair dye, hats, make-up, t-shirts, you-name-it. Fun, knowledgeable staff.

Eskandalo (623 Cahuenga Blvd., Hollywood; 323-957-0393; www.eskandal.com) Punk tees, new and vintage wear, toys, and coolest-baby-clothes-you've-ever-seen by *Motorstar Clothing* in the front, hair salon in back. Once in a while, the store is open at night and bands play.

Blest Boutique (1634 Cahuenga Blvd., Hollywood, 323-467-0191) High-end 'designer punk' clothing and jewelry, much of it made by locals. Think Malcolm McClaren & Vivienne Westwood a la their 'Sex' days. Cool handmade plates, pitchers and magnets by Skellramics. Once a month they hold "socials" at night with art shows, readings, and live performances. Save money by catching one of their killer sales.

Monkeys To Go (163 W. 2nd St., Pomona, 909-629–0377) Punk clothing, hair dye, accessories, everything — all out in the suburbs. Hit it up before a show at the Glass House.

Food Not Bombs (213-787-8654 ext. 2899; info@lafoodnotbombs.org) LA county is the nation's welfare capital, and FNB, a national revolutionary grassroots movement (big with anarchists), feeds free vegetarian food to the poor and homeless in downtown twice everyday.

Skratch (www.skratchmagazine.com) O.C.-based fanzine covering national and local punk scenes, free at shows, and available at stores.

CLUBLAND EL LAY
Clint Catalyst

El Lay's Clubland can be a frustrating dry hump or a deliciously orgasmic all-night affair. It's all about choices, baby. When visiting the city, whatever your scene, be forewarned that the usual rules do not apply here. Having a fabulous outfit, achingly beautiful bone structure, or street cred status as a nightlife celebutante in your hometown (excluding New York, the only American sibling Angelenos look up to) means nada in Hollywood, nor does being attached to someone famous. Everyone here is attached to someone famous. It's not a big deal. As a tourist, remember that this is a vacation from reality, and nightclub jaunts are merely playground attractions. As a recent transplant, however, either shut up or suck up, and pay your dues.

TO LOS ANGELES

That little tidbit tossed aside, let me give you the low-down from the highbrow to the downtown. For the unadventurous at heart, there's always the **Sunset Strip**, a winding boulevard punctuated by building-size billboards, self-consciously chic boutiques, traffic more backed-up than Jesse Helms' bowels, and $10 parking. This area is up on a hill, not underground. In other words, if salon tans and Palm Pilots are your trademarks of cool, my guess is that you won't be reading this book and will gravitate (un)naturally toward West Hollywood/Sunset Strip hangs like the exorbitantly-priced **Sky Bar** in the Mondrian (8440 Sunset, 323-650-8999), the ultra-scenester hang **Bar Marmont** (8171 Sunset, 323-650-0575) — which admittedly serves astounding dishes (the filet mignon with mashed potatoes is most God, indeed), and the **House of Blues** (8432 Sunset, 323-650-1451), a Southern chain (like Wal-Mart). I'll serve up a couple tidbits, and then move on.

The world-famous, you-know-who-died-here **Viper Room** (8852 Sunset Blvd., 310-358-1880), owned by heartthrob Johnny Depp, has been known to showcase some more-than-decent folks. Sometimes, the proverbial tables get turned. I've seen X legend John Doe open for newbie Daniel Cartier, for example. The security staff, however, is just as Look-How-Important-I-Think-I-Am as the stereotype goes. Yawn. Seating is limited, and usually reserved for mysterious guests who do not appear. One time I witnessed that handsome fellow from Everclear show up and claim his table though, so it's not full-on Snuffleufagus central. And speaking of snuffles, sniffles, whatever: the bathroom decor—slick black toilets and sleek red tile walls—beautifully brings out the bloodshot in your eyes. Viva la viva.

At the other end of the spectrum—and definitely no pot of gold — is the **Rainbow Bar & Grill** (9015 Sunset Blvd., 310-278-4232), the only venue I know in existence with a submerged stage. That's right: the band plays on a lower level than the audience. This should tip you off to the showcased "talent" and entertainingly terrifying clientele. Quite frankly, I'd forgotten about high-top Velcro-strap sneakers—especially with spandex tights tucked into them! There's no shortage of fashion "Don't" reminders at this White Trash palace, where even the most faded of rock royalty still glistens. Aqua Net Ultra Super Hold, silicon titties in snug t-shirts, and side-lace skin-tight denim will always rule. Hallemothafuckinlujah.

There's also the **Key Club** (9039 Sunset Blvd., www.keyclub.com), with its big-screen marquee outside and multiple monitors punctuating the statement indoors. But like I said: just a couple tidbits. Let's move on to the East, where things get more interesting.

The Knitting Factory (7021 Hollywood Blvd., 323-463-0204, www.knittingfactory.com) is admittedly bourgie — with the soft flicker of computer monitors illuminating the lounge area — but this place has a mighty fine sound system, decent food and bar, and a healthy scattering of chairs and tables, a welcome treat for old fogies like me who don't always want to rub crotches and hip-hop with stage-rushing teens. Many of the best shows I've seen in Hollywood have been here, from cult-status phenomenon Diamanda Galas to new school wonders The Gossip.

Down on Santa Monica Boulevard, bordering the Boys' Town territory known as WeHo, there's a new addition: **The Parlour** (7702 Santa Monica Blvd., 323-650-7968, www.parlourclub.com). Formerly a crystal meth-addled Crisco Disco, the new owner Lenny Young has spiffed the place up with gorgeous decor. Putting a new spin on its seedy reputation, the place now resembles a bordello: dark carnivalesque paintings by Dame Darcy adorn the blood-rusty walls, flickering crimson candles set the red-light district feel, thick velvet curtains frame the front room-slash-stage, and chandeliers. The bar has fucking CHANDELIERS. And just about the friendliest staff around. I've seen an adorable unsigned punk band perform here, taken in some wickedawesome (all one word, of course) spoken word, and danced my patootie off to electro and synthcore djs. Yay.

Back up in Hollywood, there's also **Blue** (1642 Las Palmas Ave., 323-462-7442), a venue comin' at ya from Mike Stewart and Bruce Perdew, promoters known for long-running club nights such as Clockwork Orange and Helter Skelter. There's dancing for the 18-and-over set — though shock-absorbent shoes are recommended for the shin-splitting concrete floor — and a restaurant serving dinner Wednesday through Saturday.

If you're old enough to drink but think dance clubs are a major yawn, two great spots to see gigs are **The Garage** (4519 Santa Monica Blvd., 323-662-6802), located in a vague area where Hollywood bleeds into Silverlake, and **Spaceland** (1717 Silverlake Blvd., 213-833-2843, www.clubspaceland.com), comfortably situated in the S.L. hipster scene.

Heading towards downtown, there's a sizzling new hotspot known as **The Echo** (1822 Sunset Blvd., 213-413-8200, www.attheecho.com), pimpin' fresh style into the area known as 'Echo Parque.' Before Ricky Martin lived *la vida loca*, a bitchen indie flick came out with the same name, and this neighborhood provided the backdrop. Now it's not just chola girl gangs who rule the turf. Ethnically diverse and always on the edge, The Echo features everything from punk rock barbeques to old school hip hop for its sexy patrons. Echo Park is burning. Say it again.

For some no-frills fun, check out **The Smell** (247 S. Main St., enter through the alley between 2nd and 3rd Sts., 213-625-4325, www.thesmell.org) an all ages, bare-bones music venue and art gallery. Smack dab in the seedy artery that is downtown Los Angeles, this locale is dank, dark, and delightfully hidden. Sure, as far as the olfactory goes, it often lives up to its name — though keep in mind that stuff that isn't cute isn't meant to be commercial; it's not cut for that particular machine. But there are other rewards. Crusty punk, death rock, dismal folk, and delightful assemblage art: this is *the* spot for all ages shows of creative types working beneath the radar and beyond the margins.

Now let's move from nightclubs to club nights. More often than not, a long-running club is a moveable beast. This one confuses many peeps. The difference between a club *night* and a club *venue* is comparable to the difference between a "house party" being thrown and the apartment where it's held. In short, don't show up at the same address on consecutive evenings and expect what you had the night before.

By that same token, it's usually best to skip the telephone calls to club venues (i.e., the buildings where the nights are housed) when scoping specific details for a club night (the party being thrown). Instead, dial a promoter's info line, scan one of the weekly papers, or look for website updates.

Working from the weekend through the week, **Cherry** (213-896-9099, www.clubcherry.com) is Hollywood's longest-running club, and with good reason. At its current locale, the newly remodeled **A.D.** (836 N. Highland), head honchos Mike Messex (d.j./heartbreaker) and Bryan Rabin (celeb party planner and high-profile man-about-town) put scads of effort into keeping up the ambience. Here you'll be sure to find top-notch go-go dancers who take pride in their positions: these bee-yatches work through several elaborate hand-crafted costumes each evening, then strip down and get sassy. Straddling the line between filthy and fierce, this place is all about the show — here I've witnessed a warped puppet act, dueling Bankhead divas, even topless aerobics in six-inch heels while eating cheeseburgers to AC/DC — and that's only what's on the stage! I'm talking Show, girl: and it's in the bathrooms, on the dance floor, hidden in enclaves: quite simply, all over the place. Be it straight, gay, rock-and-roll or new wave, Club Cherry is a great place to play.

The fourth Friday of each month is a death rock extravaganza known as **Release the Bats** (1923 E. 7th St., Long Beach, 949-263-4180, http://members.aol.com/dthrck). Held down in Long Beach but definitely worth the drive, djs Dave Grave, Dave Skott, Jeremy and Shane spin "all the doom and gloom you can possibly stand." None of the repetitive beats of contemporary club offerings under the "spooky" moniker, and absolutely all the big hair and black eyeliner. Goth is dead; long live Goth!

Twenty-four hours later, a weekly event is **Saturday Night Finger,** a Rock n' Roll discotheque djed by actor/musician Coyote Shivers (www.coyoteshivers.com). Billed as "from ABC to ZZ Top, from Iggy to Ziggy, from Marilyn Monroe to Marilyn Manson, from Riot Grrls to Spice Girls, from AC/DC to X," this sweaty, intimate affair at **Goldfingers** (6423 Yucca, Hollywood, 323-962-2913) is a low-maintenance, high-octane good time.

Bang! (www.clubbang.com) at **The Ruby** (7070 Hollywood Blvd., Hollywood, 323-467-7070) is always as packed as freeze-dried coffee, and definitely more conducive to energy. Forget the gym; just hit the dance floor and try to keep up with the 18-and-over crowd here. The ever-ubiquitous Jason Lavitt, promoter legend Joseph Brooks, and photographer-to-the-scene-queens Apollo Starr are responsible for this mod and Brit-pop party, which has chiseled such a well-defined niche it has its own CD anthology with diamond tracks from Sneaker Pimps, New Order, Charlatans UK and the London Suede.

Just in case you haven't heard, **Make-Up**

(www.clubmakeup.net) at the historic **El Rey Theater** (5515 Wilshire Blvd., LA, 323-936-4790) is a once-a-month exercise in glamorous decadence always thrown the first Saturday by the Big Daddy of SoCal promoters, Joseph Brooks, and his partner, Jason Lavitt. Jason d.j.s — and has d.j.ed — basically everywhere, and Mr. Brooks, well, he's been defining the LA club scene for over two decades. This guy has built a solid reputation for himself, and Club Make-Up is no exception to his empire. Studded with celebrity hosts, clientele in salacious costumes, and midnight tribute shows backed by the 'Gutter Gangster All-Stars' house band; Make-Up has a revolving cast of rock star players that has included everyone from Kembra Pfhaler (The Voluptuous Horror of Karen Black) to Cherrie Currie (The Runaways). Oh yeah, and the club was named 'Best Place to Bend Your Gender' by the *New Times*. Gotta love that.

Another gender-b (l) ending monthly event is **Dragstrip 66** (2500 Riverside Dr. at Fletcher, Silverlake, 323-969-2596, www.dragstrip66.com). Held the second Saturday, Dragstrip is known for its pansexual mix of patrons, who mosh and frolic in a friendly environment.

Every Saturday night is **Bar Sinister** (www.barsinister.net) at **Boardner's** (1652 N. Cherokee Ave., Hollywood, 323-769-7070), a 21-and-over gloom cookie / dark fetish netherworld that offers a welcome respite from baby bats at other Goth nights.

Sunday nights, you can go shake it at Jason Lavitt's club **Beat It!** (www.clubbeatit.net) at **The Ruby** (7070 Hollywood Blvd., Hollywood, 323-467-7070), an 18-&-over trip back to that Rubik's Cube dominated era, the, the '80s.

A cover-free, fun Monday evening can be had at the weekly 'Alternative Night' at**Rage** (8911 Santa Monica Blvd., West Hollywood, 310-652-7055), though homophobes should be warned that there's a seriously gay vibe goin' on here. On second thought, scratch that. Show up and DEAL, suckers!

For the New York celebutante feel, look no further than **Beige** at **The 360°** (6920 Sunset Blvd., Hollywood, 323-871-2995). Every Tuesday evening and without a cover charge, this penthouse club boasts the "best view in town," and there's no argument from me here. The view of its patrons is entertaining, too — though often a character study in The Cocaine Ego cut with plastic surgery.

Wednesday nights, glam rock guys Taime Down and J.D. present **The Pretty Ugly Club** (323-484-4044, www.newlydeads.com/prettyugly), a sweet-and-sour live band extravaganza at **The Dragonfly** (6510 Santa Monica Blvd., Hollywood, 323-466-6111).

Or you can "keep it real" at **Club Ghetto** (www.littleryder.com) at **Tempo** (5520 Santa Monica Blvd., Hollywood, 323-966-9555) with two floors and three rooms of inner city action, spinning hip hop, house and Latin, spanning the rough-and-ready queer papi cholo scene. Yum. If you like 'em brown, you'll be down.

A Thursday night event that's been around eons and ions is **Perversion** (www.perversionhollywood.com) at **The Ruby** (7070 Hollywood Blvd., Hollywood, 323-462-7442), a place for 18-and-olders to play on three separate dance floors of industrial, '80s and Goth.

Or 'Legal Eagles' can let it all hang out at **Lovecats**, an excellent Thursday night held at **Fubar** (7994 Santa Monica Blvd., Hollywood, 323-654-0396). D.j.ed by Adrian Barbeau and hosted by a rotating crew of drag royalty — Alexis Arquette, Billy Francesca, Choca Fresca, and the unquestionably brilliant Jackie Beat — this place spells out *fierceness* in 72-point type. And there's no cover, lover.

So… what are you waiting for? Put down this book; make up your face, and go grab the moment!

DON'T GO THERE! DO NOT GO THERE!
DID I MENTION YOOU SHOULDN'T GO THERE?
E.A. Gehman

As I write this wee paean to all that is good and holy in Los Angeles, I've lived in the **Beverly Hills Hotel** (9641 Sunset Blvd., Beverly Hills; 310-276-2251) for eight weeks. That's right, eight whole weeks. My pretty little house in the Hollywood Hills is filled with sewage and mold, but that's a story better sobbed over another time. And while I desperately miss my own home, what I want to tell you, Dear Hip Reader, is that BHH rocks.

The place is fantastic! I've stayed in hotels around the world, and some might be slicker, some might be snottier, some might be far more expensive, but with the exception of Thailand, where I had my own coterie of teenage slaves the entire time I was on the itty bitty island of Phe Du, staying in a grass cottage whose glass floor extended far over the azure waters of a very deep lagoon (and no, none of those teenagers were for sex, but thanks for thinking of me in that way), BHH is hands down the best hotel I've ever stayed in. I swear it! Even the cheapest rooms are grand and de-luxe; the food in the various restaurants is completely delish (including room service, always a tough feat to pull off); the staff is absurdly, outdatedly, otherworldy helpful and polite; the tennis courts are fast and frequently empty; and the pool is awash in both tit jobs and melanomas of all sizes, shapes and colors. In short, the place is paradise and gets massive points for being Fab-storical (that's fabulous and historical, Dear-But-Not-So-Hip Reader).

Built in the '30s, refurbished in the mid-'90s, and situated virtually in the center of Beverly Hills on Sunset Boulevard, the Pink Palace looks today much like it did back in the good old days when Gable and Lombard shagged in the bungalows, when Charlie Chaplin used to escort his barely legal babes for a quick canoodle in the bathroom by the Fountain Coffee Shop. My stay so far has included both the 2002 Grammies and Academy Awards, and wow has it been brill. For some reason this year the hotel's swamped with gangster rappers and foreign actors, so English is now not spoken in the lobby. P.Diddy was here with Lara Flynn Boyle a couple nights ago (honestly, could I make up that combo?) He went from J. Lo to L. Bo! (Hahhahahhaahha) All right, yes, yes, I was in the lobby, at the Polo Lounge drinking right before coming up here to write. (They make this delish drink called a Sidecar that has lots of liquor and sugar on the rim.) So keep the liquor factor in mind as you read, or read with a drunken slur, whydoncha; I've also brushed asses with Neve Campbell and her secret lover Selma Blair (did I say that? Cuz I meant to say John Cusack) and

Cameron Diaz and Christina Applegate, and Nicole Kidman and her sister, and Sissy Spacek and Marisa Tomei and Billy-Bob and Angelina Jolie (known among my friends as Collageena Blowme), and Kirsten Dunst and Tobey Maguire (but not together because that's over - or never was, if you believe the current line of crap they're sending out via publicists) and Britney (love ya babay, and that Timberlake lardass is a joke and a jerk so I hope ya don't care and by the time this is published surely you'll be with some other boy and maybe even have disposed of the ol' virginity), and just lots and lots of other people we need only ever refer to by their first names.... and of course all those Europeans... Jeremy Northam, Kate Winslet... and they were gabbing with Snoop Dog and Dr. Dre, with their massive posses (is that what we're calling them today?) and Destiny's Child (they don't have a posse, they have Beyonce's mom!)... And of course Russell Crowe bumped into me in the lobby this morning and while I was in the middle of thinking "Watch it, hairy pudgy fellow," he said "Excuse Me, Love" in his Aussie drawl and I realized who it was all in a fiery blushing instant and swooned inwardly as he stomped onward with two bodyguards in tow (privacy, schmivacy, Russ, baby: ya don't leave out the front doors of the hotel if you REALLY are interested in ducking the press) and lately I've seen so very much of J. Lo and her ass (they have separate suites) that I'm kind of over it (tho she does seem truly enamored of her new husband, Dance Lad).

But the truly stratospherically thrilling thing about living here is that even when NO corporate brands — ah, I mean movie stars — are around, there's always such terrific people-watching that one can sit in the lobby for hours and never get bored. It's a bottomless foray into Angeles anthropology, and a veritable demented odyssey into the dim world of eating disorders, drug/sex/plastic surgery/money addictions... And remember, you don't have to be staying at the Pink Palace to enjoy all her lovely charms. Anyone can hang in the lobby without being booted as long as you affect an air of belonging. Pretend you're a guest, or there for an event; the place does have lots of security, so don't be an ass and the guys with the wires in their ears will be cool. Sit by one of the fireplaces or over by the bathrooms — you see the entire lobby from there, including the front door. And if anyone really good has to take a whiz, you can follow them into the john for a closer look (or feel, if you're in a George Michael mood… and by the way, HIS famous bathroom, site of his untimely demise, is directly across the street from BHH, in Will Rogers Park, a lovely green enclave, even if you're uninterested in A Brief History of Entrapment and Blow Jobs in Los Angeles, and the three square feet of concrete that serve as jizz central.)

Let me wax poetic for one more moment, this time about the **Polo Lounge**: it's recently transformed from the dark lair of social-climbing agents trying to woo Vicodin-popping talent to a fun bar where the staid, formal waiters bemusedly serve youngsters looking for a little retro coolness. There's usually always a piano player singing old standards, plus the evening scene is still rife with aging millionaires and their Old School couture-wearing Hos (the kind of Hos who've had lots of "work" done). Polo playing can be a cheap night, too: one drink'll run you about eight bucks and you can nurse it for hours, and as soon as you order a drink they bring a plate of snacks — but if they bring the chips ask if they have the candied pecans and olives, they're much better.

ONE MONTH LATER

I'm still living at the hotel, still trying to write this chapter, but my life has narrowed down to this one little segment of the LA universe, and it's hard to concentrate. Last time we did this guide, I discussed sneaking onto studio lots, and gate crashing fab parties. Well, due to 9/11, those golden days are long gone. Besides, right here at the hotel there are lounge chairs, and cocktails to be imbibed. J. Lo has left the building, and now *my* ass is the reigning biggie here, thanks to eating room service every meal (they've got this outlandish blue cheese pepper bread — but I digress.) Luckily, my bum isn't quite in need of two suites yet, but it's unclear when I'll be checking out so all hope isn't lost.

Yet Pleasant bothers me daily for this fucking chapter, and all I've done is rave about the hotel. Doesn't she understand that I'm a refugee? I can't think about anything fun in Los Angeles at the moment, I'm horribly depressed because there are *fungal colonies* filling my house, and all I want to do is complain. Aha! That's it! With complaining in mind, I'm now going to discuss some places you absolutely DON'T want to visit while here in town. How's that for good guiding! You must avoid the places I'm about to mention as if they are infested with malaria, ebola, the bubonic plague — or let me be tasteless and oh-so-contemporary — anthrax.

If you've done any kind of research or even casual reading about LA before coming here, you've heard of these places, perhaps ad nauseum, and perhaps intend to include them on your itinerary. Stop this instant! Run right over to the **Polo Lounge**, have a Sidecar, and re-work your sightseeing plans. (All right all right all right, yes I *was* just down at the Polo drinking again - this time it was Naughty Girl Scouts. Repulsive, high schoolish, psycho tasty, and it furthered my goal of having an ass bigger than J. Lo's.) I've taken to popping in straight from nap time, wearing striped silk jammies with scads of pearls about my neck (rescued from the mold), a long cream-colored shearling tossed over my shoulders, spiky turquoise brocade Prada on the tootsies (Can I tell you? Two years ago,

Prada was dead over, and today, here at the ass-end of the Spring season, I feel about Prada the way I felt about blow in the '80s: so happy to see more and more of it!) And these very sick limited edition Dior sunglasses, where the D logo has flames of rhinestones flying up each earpiece. I'm a cross between Babe Paley on vitamin K and Eloise. All right, let's get down to it.

For God's sake, unless you're on the Architectural Disasters of America tour, do NOT go near the monstrosity at the intersection of Hollywood and Highland Boulevards, even if you're virtually *inside* it because you need to see the footprints at **Grauman's Chinese Theatre** (6925 Hollywood Blvd.) which also got ruined by that fucking mall, I might add. Footprints intact, vintage Chinese façade-gone. The **Hollywood and Highland Mall**, less than a year old as I write, and now home to the Academy Awards in the already-vilified **Kodak Theatre** (crap acoustics, sightlines and ticket prices) is an absolute eyesore. The place is stupid and ugly, the shops are a pathetic mishmash of high volume but useless outlets, the parking garage is an invitation to death in the event of fire or earthquake, and if you can find a public bathroom, you must be part Bloodhound; the few they have are well hidden. In the first week this place was open, everyone I know was peeing in the stairwells, myself included… let me save Plez an editor's note: her stairwell pissfest took place during the extremely long first act of The American Ballet Theatre's premiere performance of *The Nutcracker Suite*, five days before Christmas. *Well done*. And we weren't even drunk!

And lastly, reason #350 to stay away from Hollywood and Highland — this is one of the most active earthquake zones on earth, so can someone please explain to the general population why those massive white elephants are teetering on the roof? There's only one direction they're going when a big temblor hits, *and it ain't up*. To sum up, the thing is an insult to every citizen in this fine city — *nay*, (nay? I AM wasted…) an insult to anyone who's ever watched a film or dreamed of Hollywood, or even heard, in a distant land, in a foreign tongue, the mispronounced name of our fair glamouropolis, because it claims to represent Hollywood — claims to be the significant signifier for all that IS here in the center of the fictional universe. Those responsible for building it, as well as those who granted the permits to do so, should be shot, buried, then dug up and run out of town on rails.

If you've got to go to a mall while here, try **The Grove** (323-900-8000) which has attached itself to the very historic, very fun, very real **Farmers Market** on Fairfax and Third. The Grove is a little piece of Vegas right here in town, including the mini-replica of the music-cued fountain at the center, and the "historic" trolley that runs through it. It's another example of run-of-the-mill shops, but you're outdoors and the Farmers Market is right there, so you can stroll on over and experience old-time LA tourism: souvenir shop at the tiny stalls, mail home a crate of just-picked citrus fruit, eat at **Kokomo's** for a yummy breakfast, or the **Gumbo Shack** for lunch, and lots of nights there's still real old-timey music by very local, very non-hip musicians. **Kip's Toyland** is a brilliant toy store, please buy something there. Then drive north up Fairfax, have a martini at **Max's** (442 Fairfax, 323-651-4421) or **Lola's** (945 Fairfax, 213-736-5652) both bars are free of any of the attitude that has made **Skybar** such a bore. Then, take in an arty movie at **Laemmle's Sunset Five** (8000 Sunset at Fairfax, 323-650-7300). DO NOT get a snack here - instead go across the street to **Greenblatt's** (8017 Sunset, 323-656-0606), a deli with great food and an amazing wine selection.

DON'T EVEN IF THERE'S A GUN TO YOUR HEAD OR SOMEONE'S PROMISING UNLIMITED HYDROPONIC WEED go to the **Skybar** at the **Mondrian Hotel** (8440

Sunset, Hollywood; 323-650-8999) or any club or bar that has a rope in front of it that you've read about in *GQ*, *Elle*, *Bazaar*, or *Conde Naste Traveler*. Instead of the fake glam bars, try any of the little ones. There are about 150 of them, and they're like shiny baubles on a long necklace — all strung out across the sparkling dark neck of the city. **Star Shoes** (6364 Hollywood Blvd., 323-462-7827), **Daddy's** (1610 N. Vine, Hollywood, 323-463-7777), and **The Well** (6255 Sunset, Hollywood, 323-467-9355) are three that come to mind as fun and not too pretentious… The Well keeps their lights so dim on weekends that guys are always walking into the girlz room and vice versa, so that's kind of entertaining…

Do yourself the favor of a lifetime and STAY AWAY from **Universal Studios**. Not only is it overpriced and passé, but also if I'm a terrorist, this is where I'm heading with my strapped-on bomb. The place is so crowded it's difficult to walk… but easy to get pick-pocketed or groped, barring any kind of local dirty nukes activity. Instead, drive around Hollywood or the Valley until you see a film shoot taking place on the street. Repeatedly circle the block around the film shoot, and on your third or fourth pass, honk your horn. Repeat the whole sequence until one of the (hired) motorcycle cops guarding the set gives chase, and then speed away. It'll be better than any of the rides at Universal, and the neighbors being affected by the ridiculously long, noisy hours of the shoot will love you — we all hate filming in the streets, but those thoughtless bastards at the LA Film Office keep handing out permits anyway.

Don't bother to go to **Melrose Avenue**, unless you're Japanese and homesick. Then you'll think you're in Shinjuku, and the high prices and masses of expensive t-shirts will soothingly remind you of Tokyo. Instead, check out Hollywood's **Franklin Strip** between Beachwood and Bronson. Anchored by the **Bourgeois Pig** (5931 Franklin, 323-963-6366) a coffeehouse, and The **Daily Planet** (5931-1/2 Franklin, 323-957-0061) an excellent newsstand, these blocks have a bustling restaurant and bar scene, with a number of chic/funky boutiques, which stay open very late. Eat at **Prizzi's Pizza** (5923 Franklin, Hollywood; 323-467-0168) or **La Poubelle** (5907 Franklin, 323-465-0807), and then shop for beautiful shoes and purses at **Greater LA** (5915 Franklin, 323-463-5215) or amazing jewelry and handmade soaps at **Espiritu de Vida** (5913 Franklin, 323-463-0281). Right next door is the **Tamarind Theater**, see a play.

Don't go to **Griffith Park Observatory**, even if you're some psycho fan of *Rebel Without A Cause*. The place is closed for renovations until 2005. Instead, hike up **Runyon Canyon** (Fuller Avenue, a block west of La Brea, above Franklin, in Hollywood) and not only will you see the burnt remains of film star **Errol Flynn's Estate** where every rock star who grew up in LA either got high or skateboarded, but there's a nice view of the **Observatory** from the top. It's the best free workout available in the middle of the city, plus tons of opportunities for star watching. I mean, probably you won't see anything as brill as L. Bo and P. Diddy, but not everyone has my luck. And I do see Ellen Degeneres there constantly, as well as most of the casts of every sit-com on the air.

Don't bore yourself to tears at the **Los Angeles County Museum of Art** unless there's some very specific exhibit you want to see, or unless you want to know what the big controversy is about tearing the shithole down. The general collection isn't that hot, and the place itself is sprawling and confused — it's no mystery why it's slated for demo. Visionary architect Rem Koolhaas has designed the replacement, but our artistic "leaders" are currently squabbling about that, so who knows when construction will begin. (I'm gonna mention Prada again: Rem did the Prada store in NYC, go visit it at once. I feel about

Rem's designs the way I felt about sex before AIDS: the more the merrier.) Instead, go downtown to the **Geffen Branch** of the **Museum of Contemporary Art** (152 N. Central, off 1st St. between Alameda and San Pedro; 213-621-2766) It has great shows, and it's right on the edge of **Little Tokyo**, so you can pop over there for some ramen and sake or toy shopping right after. Or go to **Olvera Street** by heading north on Alameda Street. It's the site of the oldest standing house in LA and a touristy collection of old-timey Mexican crafts and souvenirs. Eat at **La Golondrina** (W-17 Olvera St., 213-628-4349), it's super yum, or at the taquito stand at the bottom of the street — the best taquitos around, with a delish guacamole sauce.

Well, that's it for me. Kinda inspired, kinda bourgeois. But whaddya expect from a drunkard who lives at the Beverly Hills Hotel? Come on by and visit. Ask for me, if ya can't find J. Lo. Things are mighty fine here in *the Hills of Bever-ly*

FETISH LA
Jayson Marston

OK: so you want to be a kinky freakazoid in LA? Here's where to start… but remember, this isn't the be-all, end-all guide to perversion in Hollywood, just a jumping- off point.

First off, it pays to advertise - and what better way to do that than by wearing the appropriate clothing? **Retail Slut** (7308 Melrose Ave., Hollywood; 323-934-1339, www.retailslut.com) is a staple of LA punk, Goth and fetish fashion. Their racks are filled with bondage pants, corsets and many one–of-a-kind designer items. They have a rainbow assortment of wigs and hair dyes, feather boas, stockings, cock rings, studded collars, patches, fanzines, even punky baby clothes, like leopard bobs or pacifiers shaped like clown-mouths or inbred redneck teeth! Browsing through the racks you will see punk rock kids, sexy professional doms, the occasional closeted gay sitcom dad (don't ask!) and that scary blonde with the great rack you see on billboards all over town, Angelyne herself. Word to the wise: be on your best behavior because the staff will kick your ass if you wise off; free beer will calm them down however.

You will also want to go shopping for some gear at **665** (8722 Santa Monica Blvd; W. Hollywood, 323-854-7276, www.665leather.com) and **Mr. S** (4232 Melrose Ave.; LA www.mr-s-leather.com) are two shops that sell only high quality toys and clothing. If you want to clamp it, catheterize it or simply chastise it these shops will have what you need. Both stock standard leather and fetish gear, and also offer some of their own creations. 665 recently expanded to 2,000 square feet, which houses their assortment of bondage/dungeon furniture. Mr. S has recently added a Madame S. collection. The Madam S line is a collaboration between designer Molly Maid of So Hip It Hurts, and the well-established Mr.S line. People who know kink and kinky fashion well staff both shops. Don't be shy - they are all experienced players and nothing can make them blush! If you are visiting LA, be sure to check out their sites beforehand and make a list of what you want, otherwise you'll be the proverbial kid in a candy store - even though the kid in the candy store probably wasn't being helped by a guy in a pair of leather chaps...

If you have a burning desire to be a porn star or simply have a burning sensation during urination, head to **AIM HealthCare Foundation** (14241 Ventura Blvd, Sherman Oaks; 818-981-5681, www.aim-med.org). AIM is where denizens of the adult film industry go to get their STD testing and treatment done. They offer HIV/STD testing and treatment as well as counseling for sexual health. AIM offers an early detection HIV test and the staff is extremely knowledgeable. The services are available for the open-minded general public as well.

If getting pierced is something you desire, I recommend

Thirteen B.C. (7661 Melrose Ave., LA, www.thirteenbc.com). This is the only shop in LA that is a member of the Association of Professional Piercers. A safe clean shop, the staff is very well-trained and has lots of experience making holes. If you want to get tattooed, try **Melrose Tattoo** (7661 Melrose Ave., LA; 323-655-4345) or **Incognito Tattoo** (750 East Colorado St., Pasadena, 626-584-9448, www.incognitotattoo.com). These shops are staffed by well-trained people, which mean you may not get the Hollywood Boulevard flash-off-the-wall prices but you *will* get quality work done. FYI: it is appropriate to tip either your piercer or tattoo artist; and haggling over prices is *not* appropriate, hey, these people aren't fishmongers!

So now you are dressed and ready for action. If you are looking for man-to-man action, **Slammer** (3688 Beverly Blvd., LA, 323-388-8040; www.slammerclub.com) is all just a regular day at Slammer. It's 2,000 feet of legal and creative erotic space. Slammer also offers HIV and STD testing on site. Any true sex pig worth his chaps in gold will be here the first night in town and every night thereafter.

As far as nightclubs and theme nights, they come and go so fast that by the time you read this, they may be done and over. One place to go looking for current fetish events is **www.fetishdomain.com**. This site lists practically everything and will pretty much dial you into the LA fetish scene. The *LA Weekly* also has club listings, events listings and personal ads, and all the stores I have listed will have fliers for different clubs, special events and play parties. Remember - play safe!

WHERE THE BOYS ARE
Barnes

I arrived in this beautiful sprawling hell fresh from the "Queercore" scene back in Toronto about six years ago. Like so many newcomers to the cruel garden that is Los Angeles, I was horrified by the pretty, plastic scene of West Hollywood and decided to settle with my Rock and Roll record collection out in funky Venice Beach, land of the freaks. I've been mapping the darker pleasures of the Los Angeles basin ever since JUST so that I could pass the secrets on to the fresh meat.

Let me play Top Daddy for a moment here, and make a suggestion. Since LA makes no sense whatsoever to the casual visitor, being a collection of cities practically indecipherable from each other when viewed from the freeway, I have always found the best approach for newcomers is to plunk oneself down and explore the madness one neighborhood at a time. There are pleasures here too numerous to mention, just waiting for those who can let go of their inner controlling bitch and are willing to play little lost lamb in this big scary city. Ready cupcake? Let's go!

SILVERLAKE

Why not start where you'll find the largest concentration of tattooed love boys? That would be the beautiful hills just east of Hollywood known as Silverlake. Homo hipsters settled in these cute Old Spanish style homes back in the golden age of Hollywood, and shared the many strollable streets with Latino families for decades. This unique combo gives the Silverlake experience a raunchy Mexico City-meets-East Village flavor, albeit with lovely tall palm trees always in view.

The perfect starting spot for a walking adventure is the corner where Santa Monica Blvd. meets Sunset Blvd., known as **Sunset Junction**. Heading both west and east from that vantage point you will be able to walk to any number of leather, porn, vintage clothing and punk rock record stores as well as cute restaurants and bars which all give you that "fags and artists reinventing the urban environment" feeling.

Make sure you have a cocktail at everyone's favorite lounge **Akbar** (4356 Sunset Blvd. at Fountain; 323-665-6810, www.akbardeluxe.com), which is both a gay-friendly straight bar and a straight-friendly gay bar... meaning anything can happen! Twenty-something smarty-pants gather with their pals to get blasted on drink specials from the sexy bartenders and groove to tunes on the hipper-than-hip jukebox in an atmosphere of Bohemian bliss.

Casita del Campo (1920 Hyperion Ave., 323-662-4255) is an old school family-style Mexican restaurant, perfect to feel the relaxed neighborhood vibes, and after dinner (or mucho margaritas) you can perhaps slip down into the cabaret theatre underneath and catch local queens performing the long-running "tranny trailer park soap opera" known as "The Plush Life" (323-969-2596, www.plushlife.com).

The Faultline (4216 Melrose Ave. at Vermont; 323-660-0889) is the most popular leather bar in SoCal thanks to its skanky mix of hot doggies, working guys and SMBD players kickin' it all together on the large outdoor patio during the slutfest known as "Sunday afternoon beer busts". And who doesn't like that? Gather there for **Club Spit** (323-969-2530, www.spitclub.com) every third Saturday of the month when Rock'n'Roll DJs Paul V. and Tom Walker hold court.

Paul and Tom's other club, **Dragstrip 66** (at Rudolpho's, 2500 Riverside Dr.; 323-969-2596, www.dragstrip66.com) happens on the third Saturday of the month and is the longest running underground party in town, featuring campy themes, cool beats and sexy boys. Those in drag get in cheaper but don't be scared if you left your high heels at home! The outdoor patio is filled chest to chest with the hottest local talent out looking to get lucky. Rudolpho's also hosts **Club 1,001 Nights** (www.club1001nights.com), a hotter-than-hot gay Arabic club that blasts Egyptian, North African, Armenian and Persian pop, and has occasional live performances by belly dancers - both male and female.

Kicks also abound at Silverlake's other leather bar the **Gauntlet II** (4219 Santa Monica Blvd., 323-669-9472) when they hold a dirty little club called **Freak Show** on the first Friday of every month. Steve and Eddie put together a veritable carnival of carnage featuring local rock'n'roll bands, fetish scenes and "performance art" (although getting a grant for an after-hours fisting scene might be a little difficult).

Nasty guys also gather after hours up the road at that flashback to '70s clone culture known as **Cuffs** (1941 Hyperion Ave., 323-660-2649), complete with poppers, cheesy dance music, and frisky patrons with sexual liberation on their minds. There is always the hugely popular sex club known as **Slammer** (3688 Beverly Blvd., two blocks east of Vermont, 213-388-8040) which reportedly has fun play spaces and hot clientele. I myself prefer the **Flex Complex** (4424 Melrose right off the 101 Freeway, 323-663-5858), a bathhouse catering to a wide variety of hot guys and featuring an outdoor pool, hot tub and garden, large well-equipped gym, and friendly patrons and staff. Those with a kink for the great outdoors should wander into lovely **Fern Dell** Griffith Park and see what local tour guides may have to offer in the way of adventure. Beware of plain-clothes and uniformed cops - this has been a cruising area for decades and is not a secret.

WEST HOLLYWOOD

O.K. since you're in LA, ya gotta visit Mecca for the small town fags filled with pretty boys and successful gay men dining, dancing and dishing on newly widened Santa Monica Blvd. between La Cienaga and Robertson. Try catching a meal at the **Cobalt Cantina** (616 N. Robertson, 310-659-8691) or the **Marix Tex Mex** (1108 N.Flores; 323-656-8800). Have coffee and dessert at **The Abbey** (684 N. Robertson, 310-289-8410) so you can feel the "lifestyle" here in the town that perfected that homo combo platter of body worship, circuit music, and rampant drug use. Unless you like Chelsea girls you better skip the bar life here though. If you insist on that, try Monday nights at **Rage** (8911 Santa Monica Blvd., 310-652-7055) where a younger mix of dancin' queens slam dance to the modern rock hit parade or further down the road at **Fubar** (7994 Santa Monica Blvd., 323-654-0396) which attracts the bright mover and shaker set all digging the rock'n'roll D.J.s and eye candy bartenders.

Older men meet the rent boys at **Numbers** (8741 Santa

Monica Blvd., 323-656-7559) and sometimes skateboard kids slouch around downstairs at the lesbian chic joint **The Normandy Room** (8737 Santa Monica Blvd., 310-659-6204) But be warned, mister, that boy with the tongue piercing and the scruffy hair just arrived from Georgia with probably a nasty Crystal habit - and a girlfriend back home - to support.

HOLLYWOOD AND BEYOND

If you really like street trade head on over to the **Spotlight**, (1601 N. Cahuenga Blvd., 323-467-2425), for a taste of what 25 bucks will get ya. (editor's note: I always described this dive as 'the place to go right when you get outta jail, when you're lookin' to get drunk, get your dick sucked and KICK SOME ASS!' And watch out for the wheelchair tranny hookers…) Friendly bartenders and the old timers at the bar will help you feel what dirty ol' Hollywood, LA's first homosexual stomping ground, was like way back in the day when John Rechy was writing *City of Night*.

The jewel of the Queer community is the **Gay and Lesbian Center** (1625 N. Schrader Blvd., 323-933-7400) with community meeting space, beautiful galleries and theatres, classrooms filled with workshops, and services for homeless and troubled youth. On site testing for HIV and other STDs are easy for walk-in patients and free at the **Jeffrey Goodman Clinic**, (1625 Schrader, 323-993-7500).

For the thrills of clubbing in the newly regenerated Hollywood nightlife, your best bet is to join the "mixed" crowd that hits the glam **Club Make-up** in full regalia every first Saturday of the month (at the **El Rey,** 5515 Wilshire 323-769-5500) or you could slum it where the suburbs invade the city at the bitchy rock'n'roll ball that is **Cherry** (836 Highland, www.clubcherry.net). After all we still like 'em young and pretty in Los Angeles.

If ghetto lovin' is more your speed, there are lots of fun places to meet a homeboy sneaking out on the "down low", like the friendly neighborhood bar **The Study** (1723 Western Ave., 323-464-9551) with its Afro-American clientele and fierce Friday night drag competitions where street kids parade endless variations of Aaliyah between booty shakin' sets by the D.J. set up on the pool table in a basement party atmosphere. Almost directly across the street is the infamous, notorious, **Coral Sands Motel**, where many a forgotten night of man-2-man action has taken place.

West Hollywood clones used to invade **Jewel's Catch One** (4067 W. Pico Blvd., 323-734-8849) back in the day but lately have left the locals alone to get crazy on the big dance floor. The **Jewel Box** in the basement is a wild little hip-hop room and one of the best places to get your freak on during the week. The fabulous get sweaty every week at **Boytrade**, (Friday nights at the **El Rey,** 5515 Wilshire) where Hip Hop and House beats keep the upwardly mobile moving. For a more relaxed vibe, try the mirrors and low ceilings of **The Lodge** (4923 Lankershim Blvd., 818-769-7722) out in the Valley, in the wilds of North Hollywood, where bad shoes and bad haircuts abound.

If it's a hot Latin night you have in mind (and Los Angeles is the largest Spanish-speaking city in the U.S.A., don't you know), you should check out the long running **Circus Disco** (6655 Santa Monica Blvd., 323-462-1291) which is a really really silly place unless you've just escaped your Catholic family in Mexico or Guatemala but a fun field trip for the uninitiated with its cruisey patio and sense of heady new freedoms in the air. Another Queer Latin club in Hollywood is the **Tempo** (5520 Santa Monica Blvd. at Western, 323-466-1094), which features a bomb ass Hip Hop night called **Club Ghetto** (www.littleryder.com, 323-966-9555) that goes off on Wednesdays.

The adventuresome might make their way to **The Score**

(107 W. 4th St., 213-625-7382) which is situated downtown near skid row and has a really great layout filled with lots of actually dangerous characters out looking for a fuck… watch your wallet and good luck, hombre.

OCEAN AND DESERT

My town Venice Beach has long been home to the hippie artists and queer freaks cruising the piers and boardwalks, after having lured folks to the beach retaining it's "anything goes" flavor. Venice started life as an amusement park back at the top of the last century. Recently things have gotten more than a little chi-chi but don't let the new influx of cell phones and sports cars fool you, it's still a thug life back in the hood! Just west of Abbot Kinney Boulevard's smart galleries and upscale restaurants, there are still boys straight off the bus who will suck your cock for a place to stay for the night.

The perfect spot for a Sunday afternoon burger would be local gay bar **The Roosterfish** (1302 Abbot Kinney Blvd., 310-392-2123) where locals eye the "townies" from WeHo on Friday nights and have the place pretty much to themselves the rest of the time. There's always a joint going around on the patio and the jukebox features everyone from the Clash to Dusty Springfield, keepin' it "real". The walk from Venice north up to the Santa Monica Pier along the beach and boardwalk is a heavy cruising zone, especially at night. If you feel like meeting a new "friend", try walking out on the sand to the lifeguard stations from the parking lots of Ocean Blvd. and remember - he has to answer truthfully when you ask him if he's a cop.

There's always a crowd squished onto the patio at the other beach bar **The Friendship** (112 W. Channel Rd., 310-454–6024) up in Pacific Palisades near Roy Rogers beach (or *Ginger* Rogers Beach, as we like to call it) where the fairies from across the city gather on sunny days to cruise, play volleyball and work on their precious tans.

While on the Westside, don't miss checking out **Highways Performance Space** (1651 18th St., Santa Monica, 310-315-1459) where Tim Miller and the ACTUP crowd started one of the nation's premiere spots to catch naked boys doing monologues about growing up queer … or someone sticking a yam up their twat. Those with a taste for younger guys should check the bookstores, hip clothing stores, and lovely cafes of Santa Monica's **Third Street Promenade** where homeless punks and trendy shoppers tend to be queer.

One of the best things about visiting LA and Southern California in general is the nearness of desert, mountains and ocean. Any number of day trips get you out into nature but if you want the "hang around and do nothing but the guy in the room next to you" vibe of Palm Springs choose **Camp Palm Springs** (www.camp-palm-springs.com or 888-2-GayFun) for its relatively inexpensive rooms and relaxed and playful patrons (army boys always free!). While you're out in the desert, check the club **Ground Zero** (36737 Cathedral Canyon, 760-321-0031) that features a Saturday night "underground" dance party. Look for a desert Daddy at the **Wolf's Den** (67625 E. Palm Canyon Dr., 760-321-9688).

That's about it for a quick'n'easy, sleazy tour around this vast playground. Oh, and remember cruising each other in cars is business as usual here so you might get picked up long before you reach your destination! That's why I always pack my leathers and an overnight bag… Happy travels, stranger!

LONG LOOSE CURLS: Lesbian LA
Lauran Hoffman

LA LESBIAN MURKY RULES & DATING DEFINITIONS

Going Out: A term used to downplay any seriousness when dating a new acquaintance. You can "go out" with as many people as you want at the same time. You may quit seeing her without much advance notice. When she later becomes popular, you can tell everyone you used to "go out" with her. She will deny it.

Hanging Out: A phrase to describe when one person likes the other more. No one gets hurt. The relationship was doomed from the start. Neither of you is wolf-like enough to make the first move. Two bunnies sliding backwards across ice.

Dating: A word that has so many meanings it's rendered meaningless. We date to see if we want to move into a duplex together and get a puppy. Or maybe we'll only have sex. Oftentimes we drive away from dinner in separate cars. You know you have a scrape on your right rear fender?

Dating Exclusively: Two dating snobs who can't commit to each other, but are definitely too good for everyone else.

Fuck Buddies: Friends who love to play Scrabble, but always forget to bring the set.

Been With: All your friends will ask you if you've "been with" her yet. You *know* what they want to know. Just give them a baffled look. Everyone will think more of you.

PLACES TO GO

Girl Bar (652 N. La Peer, West Hollywood, 877-447-5252) It isn't easy to meet girls here. For some reason, when lesbians dress up, their temperatures cool. One thing is certain; *everyone* goes to Girl Bar eventually. It's like Disneyland for dykes. I met Valerie here. She modeled for a living and was ethereally beautiful in that "I don't care about exterior beauty" sort of way. She spoke with an accent you could never place, drank vodka made from potatoes, and could dance for hours without noticing she was alone. After watching her dance eternally on one in a series of nights, I remember saying out loud to myself, "This — is not — the girl — for me." Then I got together with a shorter model I met at Girl Bar. She was actually too short to model so she called herself an actress. Justine looked more like Grace Kelly than Grace Kelly. Nice straight girl, she lived downtown. She had no car and no TV, just a ghetto blaster. She'd crank Enya and we'd go at it on her floor. She was quirky. She liked to get high and watch my TV. I loved her up and down. She loved me too much for comfort. Her own. We split up easily. Easy for her. It killed me.

The Palms (8572 Santa Monica Blvd., West Hollywood, 310-652-6188) The Palms has been a buoy of hope in a sea of lesbian venues that change more often than girls split up and get back together. I've met more girlfriends and micro-girlfriends at The Palms than any bar in Los Angeles. It is casual, unpretentious, friendly, and newly remodeled. It was the Palms Friday nightclub, called **Hot Box**. Everyone was having a blast, but suddenly I felt this gravitational pull to another end of the room. That's when I saw her. I knew she wasn't with the two chicks she was seated by because they were kissing without her.

Felt (8279 Santa Monica Blvd., West Hollywood, 323-822-3888) Felt is a restaurant/bar that gets slammed with gorgeous women on Tuesdays. Ellen Degeneres told everyone to go there. At least, that's what *she* told me one night while we were in line for the bathroom. I know, for a fact, the other miraculous ingredient to Felt's alchemy belongs to Michelle, the bartender who people follow like the Grateful Dead. Michelle could tend bar at a seedy dive in Inglewood and it would be trendy in two weeks.

Normandy Room (737 Santa Monica Blvd., West Hollywood, 310-659-6204) My posse and I always tip into the Normandy Room after eating sushi across the street at **Murakami**.

Escapades (10437 Burbank Blvd., North Hollywood, 818-508-7008) Valley clubs are great. The girls throw on some jeans, and then go out for a beer and a little pool. They might even have casual sex if you ask them nicely. "I'll have a Chopin Gimlet, and can you sugar my rim?" I ask the frighteningly sexy bartender wearing a tiny Escapades tank.

The drink arrives at the same time a dark slender angel slithers up next to me. This girl is so gorgeous I'm tempted to tell her she's smart. She speaks, momentarily breaking my blossoming crush. "Well, that looks tasty. What's in it?" she asks, dipping her finger into my glass.

My crush gains momentum. "It's a Heartbreak, want one?"

She lifts one eyebrow and smiles with the intensity of a helicopter landing on an ant. Fuck my friends. This is why I go to clubs.

Bite Down (www.bitedown.com) Not so very long ago, a roving underground club sprung up in Venice Beach. It happened twice a month and you never knew where it would be unless you received an invitation via email. Now they have their own web site that tells you where and when to find Bite Down. It's a pretty organized operation started by a couple of chicks that just wanted somewhere cool to hang out. Log on to the site and you'll be hooked up with not only the club Bite Down, but also all the other clubs in town.

Rumors (10622 Magnolia Blvd., North Hollywood, 818-506-9651) Rumors in Burbank is a hole in the wall in need of some patching. It is not the prettiest club in the world, but still it maintains a sense of pride that deserves respect.

The Oxwood Inn (13713 Oxnard Blvd., Van Nuys, 818-997-9666) The Oxwood has an old world flavor. It's kind of a mix between a hunting lodge and fish market. You can actually settle down with some cognac by the fireplace and listen to lesbian karaoke singers belt out everything from Gloria Gaynor to k.d. Lang.

PLACES TO EAT

Murakami (8730 Santa Monica Blvd., West Hollywood, 310-854-6212) Also referred to as "Lesbian Sushi," Murakami will astound you with the fantastic sushi, cooked dishes, and sheer volume of lesbians who gather every night of the week. If you don't run into at least one ex-girlfriend here I think they buy you sake. Make reservations, if you don't have them already.

Marix Tex Mex (1108 N. Flores Ave., West Hollywood,

310-656-8800) If the crowd is any indication, the best place in Los Angeles to eat and GayWatch is Marix. The indoor/outdoor design at Marix makes it an ideal place to have good food and Margarita's while still being able to get a tan and a few phone numbers. The place is always packed, so plan to wait for a table while you suck down a couple of pitchers of "Kickass" Margarita's. The most amazing thing they serve isn't on the menu. Ask for the Chipotles, a spicy soup made with chipotle peppers, rice, and your choice of shrimp or eggs.

Benvenuto (8512 Santa Monica Blvd., West Hollywood, 310-659-8635) Every restaurant should serve free crispy bread with a garlic and oil dipping sauce before you've even ordered! The fact that there are more adorable gays and lesbians than any poolside party at David Geffen's makes this place godlike. Mix that with great food, reasonable prices, and charming ambience, you have the most frequented Italian restaurant in WeHo.

Skewers (8939 Santa Monica Blvd., West Hollywood, 310-271-0555) This popular restaurant is lesbian-owned, friendly and fabulous. Don't be misled, not all the food is on skewers, which is lucky for the Babaganooch.

OTHER STUFF

Sisterhood Bookstore (1351 Westwood Blvd., Westwood, 310-477-7300) For those who like to meet more literate types, or even if you just like to rub elbows with fellow lesbians while browsing through those heavy things with pages, Sisterhood is the place to go. Not only do they have the greatest name, the staff is always happy and willing to please. The space is casual and cozy, perfect for settling down with a girl, a book, or both. Be sure to call them for a listing of special events such as readings, meetings, rap groups, book clubs, etc.

Dog Park The dog park puppies dream about is located in Venice, at the corner of Main St. and Westminster St. Maybe it's the abundance of tennis balls, the ample parking or the divine location, but lesbian ladies are always swarming the place. Sometimes they even forget to bring their dogs. I once saw some cutie with her cat on a leash. Guess she'd take whatever attention she could get. A dog park is an ideal place to pick up. You ask the girl, "How old is your dog?" She answers, "I'm single." Bam, you're in a relationship.

HOORAY FOR HOLLYWOOD!
(AND LOS FELIZ, TOO)
Pleasant Gehman

Hollywood and Los Feliz (also known unofficially as East Hollywood) are full of fun things to do: tons of rock clubs, theaters, boutiques, restaurants and souvenir shops... not to mention parks, landmarks, and serendipitous diversions. Hollywood used to be a seedy and forgotten ghost town, though for the past couple of years it has been undergoing extensive urban renewal, which makes locals like me a little ambivalent. The upside is that many historic buildings have been given facelifts. Art Deco masterpieces **The Pantages Theater** (6233 Hollywood Blvd., 323-365-5555) which hosts Broadway musicals, and the **Egyptian Theater** (6212 Hollywood Blvd., 323-466-FILM) have never looked better. **The Pig and Whistle** (6714 Hollywood Blvd., 323-463-0000), a Raymond Chandler-era restaurant and watering hole, has been restored to its original splendor after years of being literally walled up inside a trashy pizza place.

A lot of new cute stores, cafes and bars have opened, too. **The Knitting Factory** (7021 Hollywood Blvd., 323-463-0204) is a thinking person's nightclub, with great food, an internet café, and two showrooms featuring acts ranging from touring bands to underground films to spoken word. Another good thing is that new-ish subway system also makes it possible to get from Hollywood to Downtown LA in about fifteen minutes. On the other hand, there is always extensive construction going on, with seemingly no end in sight, and parking has gone from being a problem to being a migraine headache. Malls,like the gigantic new one at **Hollywood And Highland** (which houses the state-of-the-art **Kodak Theater**, new home of the Oscars) and the monstrosity that now surrounds the Pacific Theater's funky vintage **Cinerama Dome** (Sunset Blvd. Between Vine and Ivar) are springing up like mushrooms. Everything is getting very corporate and commercial. Some of the new stuff is great - like the **Hollywood Farmers Market** (open until 1 pm, every Sunday, Ivar and Selma Avenues, Hollywood). Here, you can get fresh produce dirt cheap, eat excruciatingly mouth-watering tamales, and shop at little stands that sell everything from homemade olives or freshly baked bread to vintage clothing, crafts, vitamins, jewelry and candles. While you're walking around (rare for natives!) it's still fun to amble along the Walk of Fame and try to find your favorite stars (everyone from Lassie to Marilyn Monroe to the Three Stooges) along the pink and black granite. At its western end, just east of La Brea, you can still enjoy all the historical hand and footprints in the courtyard of **Grauman's Chinese Theater Complex** (6925 Hollywood Blvd., 323-464-8111) - the front part of my platform shoes fit perfectly into Trigger's horseshoes! And they show current features for bargain prices during matinee hours. The interior of the main theater is gorgeous, all Chinois, red lacquer, coiling dragons, and oriental chandeliers.

Walk a little further east past the multitude of souvenir shops, and you will come to **Frederick's of Hollywood** (6608 Hollywood Blvd., 323-466-8506), the famous lingerie store. The exterior is purple and lavender, a 1920s Egyptian-moderne dream, and the interior is a stripper's wet dream. They also have a lingerie museum inside, with scanties from celebs ranging from Raquel Welch to Madonna, as well as old stripper costumes. Continuing in the underwear vein, at the corner of Hollywood and Wilcox is **Playmates of Hollywood** (6438 Hollywood Blvd., 323-464-7636), an ooh-la-la emporium that also features costumes year round, marabou boas, pasties, clubwear, great purses and rhinestone jewelry. The staff is all young and hip, and the owner's uncle, Michael Atti, is a Buddhist monk. No kidding - this may be the only lingerie store in the world that features glittery statues of Hanuman and a meditation center upstairs. Just down the street, at the corner of Hollywood and Ivar, is **Hollywood Wigs**, where you can buy all manner of hairpieces (in rainbow shades to match the slutty undies you just bought) as well as $1 false eyelashes. Need I mention that this place is a haven for drag queens? Watching the regulars try on falls is like watching a Vegas-style floor show!

One block down from the wig store, at the famed corner of Hollywood and Vine, is **Deep** (1707 North Vine, 323-462-1144) which is a sprawling, upscale nightclub whose main theme is voyeurism - there are two-way mirrors, private rooms, champagne and crème brulee, as well as very easy-on-the-eyes, underwear-clad male and female go-go dancers writhing around behind the bar as well as on a plexiglass ceiling. No wonder Hugh Hefner and Heidi Fleiss were checking the place out the minute it opened! Just north of Deep on Vine is **The Palace**, where they used to shoot *Queen For A Day* but now feature all sorts of dj clubs and concerts - check the *LA Weekly* for listings. Across the parking lot from the Palace, in an unmarked storefront is the **Earl Jeans Outlet**, a very well-kept secret where you can get those awesome-fitting *hideously* expensive jeans for about thirty bucks, because they're "irregular". This usually means that, like, a thread or two is missing. They're open daily, but only take cash. On the opposite side of the street is the famous landmark **Capital Records Tower**. You probably won't see any rock stars here, but you will at **Jumbo's Clown Room** (5153 Hollywood Blvd., 323-666-1187) a hole-in-the-wall strip joint where Courtney Love used to work before Hole and Kurt. This has always been a hot spot for rock'n'roll types, (Lemmy from Motorhead practically lives there) and features a mini-stage (complete with pole) and girls stripping to shit like The Cramps or Prodigy. Another larger club is **Cheetah's** (4600 Hollywood Blvd., Los Feliz; 323-660-6733) which has probably the best and prettiest dancers working. The pole work you see here is amazing because most of the women are professional dancers in between 'regular' dance-gigs. The atmosphere is friendly, the tunes are trendy, and the drinks, though a bit pricey, are strong.

As far as "regular" bars go, there are tons, and many feature live music. A few good spots are **The Blacklite** (1159 N. Western, 323-469-0211) which used to cater mostly to transsexual prostitutes but has become a divey hipster hotspot of sorts, and **The Room** (1626 Cahuenga, just south of Hollywood, in the back alley, 323-462-7196) which features **Dirty** , a hip rock club with local celebutante Christina Carey spinning discs on Tuesdays. **The Lava Lounge** (1533 N. La Brea Ave., north of Sunset, 323-876-6612) not only makes tropical drinks loaded down with fruit and parasols and plastic monkeys, but also has live entertainment. The decor is *tres exotique*, the Rat Pack would be right at home here. On the Boulevard itself (just west of Argyle, next to the Pantages Theater) is **The Frolic Room** (6245 Hollywood Blvd., 323-462-5890), a tiny hole-in-the-wall with a vintage Hirschfeld mural taking up one whole side, and a great jukebox. The nearby **King King** (6555 Hollywood Blvd., 323-960-9234) used to be a hoppin' club in the '80s, and has just re-opened. Featuring hot blues, Latin jazz, ska, rockabilly and bebop as well as funny theme nights like "Sexy Executive" (dress the part and get in free!). Everyone is happy this place has made a comeback

Another popular bar - heck, the entire restaurant is a landmark - is **El Coyote** (7312 Beverly Blvd., west of La Brea, 323-939-2255) which has killer margaritas, and waitresses that dress up in hoop-skirted flamenco garb and make-up that would make Divine green with envy. The decor is pure camp: velvet paintings, chandeliers shaped like bunches of grapes... some people say that the food leaves a little to be desired, but the general consensus is that after one or two of the margaritas, who cares? On a macabre note, this bistro (open for the past half-century) was also the site of Sharon Tate's last meal, before the Manson murders. An exotic place to eat is **Moun of Tunis** (7445-1/2 Sunset, near Gardner, 323-874-3333) a Tunisian and Moroccan restaurant, full of tented private rooms, incense, and low lights. You get your hands washed by a server, lay back on couches, and eat North African cuisine with your fingers while watching a belly dancer perform. The likes of Sharon Stone, Ethan Hawke, Johnny Depp, and The Rolling Stones are regulars here. Private rooms are available at no extra cost - just call ahead to reserve.

Directly next door is **Guitar Center**, with its own little rock'n'roll Walk of Fame, where you can see the handprints of legends like Ozzy Osbourne and Alice Cooper. If you're more into gangsta rap, R&B or hip hop, you might wanna check out

Roscoe's House of Chicken and Waffles (1518 N. Gower, north of Sunset, 323-466-7453) when bars close or on a Sunday morning. This is more an experience than a restaurant. It's a teeny-tiny place loaded with tables where they serve unbelievably fattening, amazing soul food: chicken and waffles, of course, but also greens, black-eyed peas, chitlins, etc. There's usually a line to get in and tons of limos outside. Everyone is yakking on cell-phones and checking their Palm Pilots, the women all look like Lil' Kim, Beyonce Knowles and Mary J. Blige, and come to think of it, they're probably not clones, but the real thing!

Along these lines, there are other restaurants that serve as places to see and be seen, all of which have been around so long they're not 'flavor-of-the-month' but established, well-known pieces of Hollywood history. **Joseph's Greek Cafe** (1775 Ivar, between Franklin and Hollywood, 323-462-8697) is THE place for "power" brunches in an unpretentious atmosphere for everyone from screenwriters to rock stars. Slurp lentil soup or lick tzatsiki off your fingers while trying not to stare at Johnny Knoxville or Marilyn Manson. They just did extensive renovations and opened a marvelous bar that's a hopping nightspot, too.

Over in Los Feliz is **Home** (1760 Hillhurst, 323-669-0211) which serves American food - meatloaf, burgers, breakfasts, and huge salads - in a gorgeous, jungle-like garden patio. **Miceli's** (1646 Las Palmas, just south of Hollywood Blvd., 323-466-3438) and **Palermo's** (1858 N. Vermont, Los Feliz) are both age-old, awesome Italian restaurants, with heaping portions, maps of Italy on the walls, and lots of cops chowing down, which is always a sign of killer food! Miceli's has a piano bar with live lounge music and special jazz shows with guest singers I've seen Julia Roberts there twice, for whatever that's worth... A well-kept neighborhood secret is **Huston's**

Texas Pit Bar-B-Que (1620 Cahuenga, 1/2 block south of Hollywood Blvd.; 323-464-3972). *Everyone* eats here, sitting at Formica tables, with coleslaw and hot sauce dribbling down their chins. It's awesome! They say there's magic in Hollywood, and across the street from Houston's, **Panpipes Magical Marketplace** (1641 Cahuenga, 323-462-7078, www.panpipes.com) carries occult books, candles, tarot cards, talismans, etc. they also hold workshops and do card readings.

For a panoramic view of the famous Hollywood Sign, drive north on Beachwood from Franklin Avenue, and it will be there, right in front of you, rising from the hills. You can't get up to it without hiking for, like, three hours up through brush and fire trails (this is definitely not recommended, not just because of snakes and bad terrain but because you'll probably get popped for trespassing) but you can turn left onto Ledgewood Drive, then right on DeRonda and continue up, up, up, to a great view point, suitable for a Hollywood photo-op.

If you want to get all cowboys, mosey on up to **Sunset Ranch** (3400 Beachwood, 323-469-5450) and go horseback riding through the hills of Griffith Park. They rent horses (for riders of all levels) for $20 an hour, and offer a terrific hour and a half moonlight ride ($40) down the hill into Burbank, culminating in a Mexican dinner; they also offer private night rides with a ten-person minimum and riding lessons.

The Beachwood Cafe is located on Beachwood just inside the gates of Hollywoodland (twin stone towers left over from the '20s when the entire area was real estate development - later they dropped the 'land' and it became plain old Hollywood). This coffeeshop is homey and cute, with gigantic portions of comfort food, malts, a few concessions to nouvelle cuisine, and patrons who "take meetings" in expensive sweats, fresh from yoga class.

Another Hollywood landmark is **The Derby** (4500 Los

Feliz Blvd., at Hillhurst, 323-663-8979), which used to be one of the Brown Derby restaurants, though not the one shaped like a hat. The Derby is an elegant, airy club which hosts swing dancing most nights to a live band (call for the free dance lesson schedule). They make mean martinis, and the adjacent restaurant **Louise's Trattoria** (4500 Los Feliz, 323-667-0777) features reasonable prices, scrumptious California Italian food (with an extensive veggie menu) that can be ordered into the club.

Don't even think of going there unless ya look the part. If you need some ink to get you're hip-quotient up to speed, call Bob Roberts, his son Charlie, and Joey Vegas at **Spotlight Tattoos** (5859 Melrose Ave., 323-871-1084). Elevating tattoos to fine art, this is one of the oldest established shops in the area, and they do fine work. An appointment is necessary, however.

There are a couple of neighborhoods that'd be good for a full afternoon or evening date where you won't need a car - everything you could possibly want to do is right there within a couple of blocks. One is the **Franklin Strip** - Franklin Ave. between Tamarind and Canyon Drive. There is the tiny **Tamarind Theater** (5927 Franklin, 323-465-7980) which hosts comedy and one-act plays; **Birds** (5925 Franklin, 323-465-0175), a great place for chicken, wraps, and snacks with a full bar and a hopping neighborhood scene after dark; **Pimai Thai Cuisine** (5833 Franklin Ave, 323-461-7841); **Holly Hills Video** (1931 N. Bronson Ave, 323-463-1750); and **Counterpoint Records** (5911 Franklin Ave., 323-469-4465), which houses a huge stock of new and used vinyl, CDs, cassettes, and books. The adjacent **Harmony Gallery** features art by people like ex-Warhol superstar Mary Woronov, and regular readings by the likes of Lydia Lunch, Jerry Stahl, Lily Burana, and touring authors. Very cool. There's also **Holly Hills Cleaners & Laundry** (1925 N. Bronson Ave., 323-469-1466); **Victor's Spirits** (1915

N. Bronson Ave., 323-464-0275), a gourmet wine shop that also delivers; a Laundromat with where actors are constantly reading their sides, and **The Inn Place** (1923 N. Bronson, 323-462-1413), a tasty budget-priced Chinese joint. As if that weren't enough, across the street is a sprawling, Gothic castle that houses Scientology, if you think you may want to join up.

The other cool strip to wander is Vermont Avenue between Hollywood and Franklin, in Los Feliz. A really popular hang here is **Fred's 62** (1850 N. Vermont, 323-667-0062), a retro-looking diner that serves really healthy, vaguely Asian-tinged coffeeshop food and stays open to the wee hours. One of the best vintage shops on this strip is **Squaresville** (1800 N. Vermont, 323-669-8464), which is always getting new stock in and does trades as well as selling and buying clothes. **Y-Que** (1770 N. Vermont, 323- 664-0021) is a hot little knick-knack shop with objets d'art, handmade and ethnic jewelry, stickers, candles, calendars, soap, T-shirts, etc. - a good place for gift-buying. The **Los Feliz Theater** (1822 N. Vermont Ave.) has current movies with bargain matinees as well as art films, and right next-door is **Mako**, a dirt-cheap, scrumptious Japanese restaurant. **Skylight Books** (1816-1/2 N. Vermont, 323-660-1175) is huge and sunny, with mind-boggling selections from the classics to hard-to-get fanzines. They regularly host high profile readings and booksignings from amazing authors like Hubert Selby, Jr. and Eileen Myles, and even musical events. And right next door is the **Skylight Theater**, where you can see plays. **The Dresden Room** (1760 N. Vermont, 323-665-4294) was popularized by the movie *Swingers* but has been a popular wateringhole since the early '60s, and still features the campy husband and wife duo of Marty and Elayne, who wear matching his'n'her sparkly outfits and do lounge numbers and showtunes five nights a week. The bar area is cozy and always jammed, and there's a futuristic dining room in the back with plush, off-white tuck'n'roll booths where you can order the Dresden's cholesterol-laden but invariably delish fare - things like deep-fried stuffed mushroom caps. Almost next door is **Mondo Video** (4328 Melrose, near Normandie, 323-953-8896), the best - and probably only - video store in town that specializes in stuff like splatter flicks, blaxploitation films, crappy vintage made-for-TV movies, porn with dwarves, and all-time cheesy cinema. Sometimes in the summer they turn the back alley into a BYOB "drive-in" and screen movies on the side of the building. Go in at any random time of day and meet washed-up porn stars and watch sleazy Hammer horror flicks or evangelist videos. They also have an impressive collection of hard-to-find CDs, scary vinyl, black velvet paintings, and used clothes. Along this part of Vermont there's also a post office, a couple of tattoo shops, a Greek place, and a great taco stand/carwash with a Starbucks right near it. And just down the street is **Barnsdall Park**, which in addition to nice grounds and art galleries, hosts kids classes and performance programs, has an auditorium, and Frank Lloyd Wright's magnificent Hollyhock House. Tired from running around? I saved the best for last. My favorite thing on the face of the earth... well, one of them, anyway... is the rosewater sorbet at **Mashti Malone's** (1525 N. La Brea Ave., Hollywood, 323-874-0146). This Persian ice cream parlor makes their own frozen delicacies - creamy confections of pistachio, coconut, chococlate and nougat, you name it. But their rosewater sorbet is like eating a mouthful of chilly, perfumed crystal flowers. You pour sour cherry syrup on it, and squeeze in a few drops of fresh lemon, and you'll be in heaven, I swear.

Please believe that I could go on and on about things to see and do in Los Feliz, let alone Hollywood. You just gotta hit the streets. Now get your explorations started!

SOMEONE LEFT THE CAKE OUT IN THE RAIN:

MacArthur Park, Koreatown

& Downtown LA

Pleasant Gehman

Y'ever watch those old re-runs of *Adam Twelve* or *Dragnet*? Even back in those days, the areas mentioned here were kinda… not a good idea at night. The only reason anyone'd go there after dark would be to buy drugs in MacArthur Park - but the Rampart Scandal sort of messed that scene up. Instead of makin' like The Artist Formerly Known As Prince's sidekick Appollonia Kotero, who made headlines with a MacArthur Park crack bust, you could visit the slightly divey **HMS Bounty** (3357 Wilshire Blvd., 213-385-7275). They do food, serve strong cocktails, have a great jukebox, and bartenders and waitresses that look like perfectly preserved wax-works.

This area of town was popular with the boho set for its cheap rent, though it's quickly becoming gentrified - which means expensive. One of the perks of this gentrification is that many of the historic Art Deco buildings are being refurbished, and at twilight, their restored neon signs silhouetted against the pink skies and palm trees is really a sight. Taking a walk down **Alvarado Street between 6th and 8th** on a Sunday afternoon is a must. There are multiple swap meets within a block selling new, not vintage merchandise. Mostly, they sell trendy knock-offs, Chinese and Japanese toys, piñatas, hair accessories, and cheap electronic stuff. They're all like glorified 99-Cent stores. Just as worthy of mention are the small 'Centro Naturisto' or 'Botanica' stores where, besides other religious paraphernalia, you can buy Love Potion, Good Luck, Buddha, Good Fortune or Gambler's Luck in spray cans, not to mention Keep Away Evil Spirits Floor Wax or Essence of Bend Over Oil!

Refreshment is guaranteed by the fruit stands dotting the street, where you can get handcarved mango roses, *jugos naturales* (fresh fruit juice) or little plastic packets of cucumber, mango and watermelon, favored with chile, salt and lemon. Then there's always **Langer's Deli** (704 S. Alvarado, 213-483-8050), a neighborhood staple for over fifty years, serving pastrami and French Dip brisket sandwiches: big whopping things with sides of slaw or potato salad and pickles, about $8 each. If you call ahead and are in a car, the staff of Langer's will provide curbside service, literally running the food out to your vehicle. Now, that's LA!

On Sundays, relax on the **Pedalo Boatride** (213-383-0496) on MacArthur Park Lake, just south of Wilshire Boulevard. On any other day, a giant water fountain is spewing in the middle of the lake, but it's turned off for the Pedalo business on Sundays, effectively preventing any water wars or soaking wet danger zones. If you've got a date, to turn this into a truly romantic ride, you may want to consider having some Valiums on hand, since the speaker-amplified, religious rantings of several 'Jesu Cristo is Lord' groups are in competition with each other as to who can spread the word in the most passionate, convincing, and loudest way.

There are a lot of cool places to eat in this neck of the woods - where you can eat and drink to your heart's content for a reasonable price. Try **Soot Bull Jeep** (3136 W. 8th St., 213-387-3865) for awe-inspiring Korean barbeque, each table featuring a grill so you can cook your own meat, which they bring to the table in marinated heaps on huge platters, or **Taylor's Steakhouse** (3361 W. 8th St., 213-382-8449) where you can pretend you're a businessman, chomp on porterhouse steaks and guzzle martinis, engulfed in a fat, high-sided tuck'n'roll booth. Or head to **Chinatown** (Broadway near Alpine, Downtown) where there are many great restaurants, some really kooky, tacky bars, and lots of "alternative" art galleries nestled in among the souvenir shops. **Lowenbrau Kellar** (Beverly Blvd. just east of Virgil, 213-382-5723) is a cavernous Teutonic grotto with full suits of armor, heavy wooden furniture, and aging frauleins who serve groaning plates of steaming sauerbraten and humongous steins of German beer. If you're really in the mood for adventure, head east on Sunset Boulevard, (which turns into Caesar Chavez near Olvera Street - also a fun way to spend an afternoon) past the Terminal Annex Post Office, and drive across the bridge. Try any one of the small taquerias there for a cheap and usually amazing meal.

OTHER POINTS OF INTEREST AND SHOPPING

Museum of Contemporary Art /MOCA (250 S. Grand Plaza, 213-626-6222) Collections of modern work by prominent national and international artists, housed in a building designed by Japanese architect Arata Isozaki.

Japanese-American National Museum (369 E. 1st St. at Central Ave., 213-625-0414) Traditional arts and crafts, artifacts, photos, etc.

Little Tokyo (adjacent the museum) A plethora of great

sushi bars, sake bars, souvenir shops (kimonos, tea sets and the like) plus amazing toy shops with items like Godzilla lighters that spit flames, Power Puff Girls and Hello Kitty paraphernalia, stickers, etc.

Museum of Neon Art/MONA (501 W. Olympic at Hope St., 213-489-9918) Neon, electric and kinetic art, plus a permanent collection of gorgeous signs from the 1920s-1960s.

USC Performing Arts (213-740-7111) Concerts, stage productions, small theater pieces, ballet, even info on football and basketball games.

Watts Towers (1727 E. 107th St., east of Willowbrook, 213-847-4646) Not really downtown, but just a hop, skip, and a jump away by the freeway - incredible towers made from junk immortalized in countless movies. For over 33 years, Simon Rodia built these structures from salvaged steel rods, pipes, bed frames, cement, pottery, shards of glass, and over 70,000 seashells. A small gallery is open Tues.-Sat., 10 a.m. - 4 p.m. Also the site of the Watts Summer Games.

The Jewelry District (on and around Broadway, near 7th St, Downtown) Rows of stores selling gold, silver, precious and semi-precious loose stones and jewelry, all at really ridiculously low, wholesale prices. And while you're down there, check out the incredible architecture on the old movie palaces and vaudeville houses, like **The Orpheum** and **The Palace**, both of which screen the occasional film or sometimes have concerts.

The Alley (Santee St. between Maple and Olympic) Every kind of trendy fashion, shoes, T-shirts, costume jewelry, make-up, kiddie clothes: usually of dubious quality, but dirt cheap; fun, bustling walking street, bargains galore. Also nearby are scores of discount fabric and trimming stores; try **Berger's Beads** or **Bohemia Crystal** if you're feeling like getting crafty and going crazy with a Bedazzler. On Maple, there's blocks of discount shoe - emporiums where you can get trendoid stuff like lime green velvet platforms for, like, fifteen bucks a pair, or brand name shoes (shit like Skechers, Volatile, Chinese laundry, etc.) for less than half of what you'd pay at the mall.

LA BOHEME:

SILVERLAKE & ECHO PARK

Pleasant Gehman

As far as neighborhoods go, Silverlake and Echo Park have always had strong personalities, and a uniquely "City of Angels" feeling. Charming and hilly, with winding streets a-bloom with tropical flowers and palm trees, littered with quaint 1920s bungalows, these two Eastside districts have historically been a bohemian enclave, as well as a melting pot of Asian, Armenian and Central American families, many of whom have lived there for generations. Throughout the years many residents have been labeled "low income" and though there's always been a gang presence, there has also been a strong sense of community and neighborhood pride. More recently, Silverlake and

Echo Park became synonymous with words like "trendy" and "cutting edge" because of the scads of artists and musicians that live there. They moved in because rent was cheap, and started redoing little storefronts into hip boutiques and restaurants, and before long, everyone else caught on to the entire district's appeal and both 'hoods prices have skyrocketed.

The charm and allure of this area just west of Chinatown has been credited to the seemingly endless swell of coffeehouses, galleries, nightclubs, book and antique stores, but in spite of all these great places (and there are many) a lot of the charm of Echo Park and Silverlake lies in the past. Amazing architecture, from ornate Victorian mansions to campy 1950s dingbat apartments makes every hidden avenue drip with character. You can put on any *Little Rascals* episode and see the streets of Silverlake and Echo Park; and the hillside staircases once used for gags by Laurel and Hardy and the Three Stooges are still intact. A fairytale bridge on Franklin and St. George, and a larger one on Hyperion and Rowena, both look as though they were lifted from old movie sets. Film companies like Selig, Bison, and Mack Sennett's Keystone shot here frequently. One of Walt Disney's first studios was located here, and everyone from silent star Pola Negri to Erroll Flynn to Charles Bukowski and Beck has lived here. On a summer day, the neighborhoods seem to have their own special light. There is nothing better than standing in the middle of Angeleno Heights, looking out over the 101 Freeway and savoring the view. On clear days, you can see from East LA to the ocean, and it will make you appreciate the true beauty of Los Angeles.

Millie's (3828 W. Sunset, 323-664-0404) is a tiny vintage-style diner with great breakfasts (try the Devil's Mess or the Jackie G) and marvy homemade fare. The staff is usually artists or band-members, and the patrons all have Krazy Kolor hair, sunglasses, lots of tattoos and are about to be The

Next Big Thing. People sit at the tables outside and chainsmoke, joining each other's conversations. Brian the dishwasher sometimes comes out and hands everyone a piece of bubblegum. The music blasting ranges from punk to Hank Williams to Arabic pop. Nothing says Silverlake like Millie's. Way crowded weekend noon/brunch time. Just next door is **Dixie Fried** (3530 Sunset, 323-664-9364), a fun little boutique that stocks to-drool-over naughty chick clubwear and vintage clothes; and **American Electric Tattoos** (3532 Sunset, 323-664-3530) where artist Craig Jackman will regale you with crazy stories as he inks your flesh. Check out his Keane paintings and taxidermy collection! Down the street at the **Silverlake Lounge** (2906 Sunset at Silverlake) third-world trannies and Banda cowboys meet hipsters for drinks, alternative rock shows and sometimes a drag revue. If you're looking for an equally crazy but slightly more civilized mix of subcultures, try **Akbar** (4356 W. Sunset, 323-665-6810) which has to be the grooviest east side watering hole with a fantastic jukebox, vaguely Middle Eastern decor, and a fun crowd ranging from queer club kids and scene-fixture artists to curiosity-seeking Westsiders. A sardine-packed nightmare on the weekends, there's usually a line to get in and once inside, you can't move. But they make up for it on Mondays, where Happy Hour prices are in place all night. And how can you go wrong at **The Red Lion Tavern** (2356 Glendale Blvd., 323-662-5337) with steins 'n' frauleins, kraut 'n' sausage, suits of armor, red tuck 'n'roll leather booths, and dark beer galore? Get out yer lederhosen and go wild, schatzi!

For some, the German thing is kinky, for others, it's a little more complicated. Know what a "plushie" is? Someone with a sexual fetish for plush toys and cartoon characters. One of the most plushie-friendly places in Silverlake has to be **Crest On Sunset** (3725 Sunset Blvd., 323-660-3645, www.crestonsunset.com).

This friendly coffeeshop serves massive portions of food with movie buff names like the Gloria Swanson Salad and the Mildred Pierce Omelet. The patrons all look like leather daddies or club kids, and the décor is, well… a little outré. There's a menacing Chuckie doll sitting on the soda machine, random stuffed animals and plush toys laying on the room dividers or the edges of the booths, and all the waiters seem to be writing your orders with psychedelic marabou-fluff pens.

Just down the street is another enclave of insanity disguised as a Mexican restaurant, **El Conquistador** (3701 Sunset, 323-666-5136). Always decorated in a luxuriant, fantastically tacky way, El Conquistador has great food, but is known for their killer - as in lethal - Margaritas. Try one, that's all you'll need. Echo Park's **Mae Ploy** (2606/8 Sunset, 323-353-9635) serves Thai-Chinese food that always hits the spot, and if you like carne asada, the **Mexican Ranch market** directly across the street marinates their own, which you can buy by the pound, take home, and barbeque to perfection. Cajun restaurant **Cirxa** (3719 Sunset, 323-663-1048) does scrumptious hush puppies, Creole Etouffee, catfish, gumbo, etc. It's a nice place dine in, but they also do take out and catering.

Both sides of Sunset Boulevard right around this part have a number of interesting little stores. Check out **Ragg Mopp** (3816 Sunset, 323-666-0550) for reasonably priced, awesome vintage jewelry, shoes clothes, knick-knacks and some furniture. They also have a gallery showing emerging local artists. **Pull My Daisy** (3908 Sunset, 323-663-0608) sells stuff by local designers, cards, and some vintage threads, while the **Den of Antiquity** (3936 Sunset, 323-666-3881) has an ever-changing collection of furniture and bric-a-brac, from Atomic Age coffee tables to paintings, lamps, and antique posters from China. **Floyd's Industrial Goods** (3822 Sunset, 323-664-8121) stocks antique hardware and cool weird stuff. There are also quite a number of antique stores, with everything from home furnishings to costume jewelry, clothes, signs, etc., a few blocks east on Sunset in Echo Park, between Mohawk and Alvarado streets.

This strip cooks at night, too with **The Echo** (1822 Sunset, 213-413- 8200) a former Guatemalan restaurant that has great live bands and deejays and also houses the Echo Park Social Club, a weekly meeting of artists and musicians. Down the road a piece is **The Short Stop** (1455 Sunset, 213-482-4942) which used to be an LAPD hang until the infamous Rampart Scandal put an end to all that. Now, it's owned by hipsters - ex-Afghan Wig Greg Dulli is a partner - and is packed with alt-rock types on the make, but it's still a good place to go after a baseball game. If you want to take in a game at **Dodger Stadium**, or take a tour of the place, call the **LA Dodgers Hotline** (323-224-1448).

The **Casbah Café** (3900 Sunset, 323-661-7000) not only makes yummy North African mint tea and thermonuclear Turkish coffee, they'll feed you with sandwiches, salads and desserts, and tempt you with fluffy Turkish towels, Moroccan scarves, embroidered pajamas, and little home accessories. **Now and Again** (3815 Sunset, 323-662-4338) sells eclectic furnishings and lamps, while **Mollycoddle** (3820 Sunset, 323-664-8778) stocks adorable baby clothes that look old-fashioned but are new, gifts, cards and jewelry.

SUNSET JUNCTION

The area of Sunset Boulevard between Fountain and Santa Monica Boulevard, just East of Los Feliz and just west of Silverlake proper, is known as Sunset Junction. There are tons of cool stores, bars and restaurants, all open day or night. **The Vista Theater** (4473 Sunset Dr., 323-660-6639) offers first-run movies at discounted prices, and is the home of the fledgling

Silverlake Film Festival. Other points of interest include **Tang's Donuts**: where old men from near-eastern countries play endless chess games; **El Cid**: tasty, if somewhat pricey, Spanish food, with nightly flamenco shows featuring the hottest dancers, musicians, and singers. This building was also one of Hollywood's first soundstages. **Tsunami** is a cool coffeehouse; **Circus of Books**: all the porn that's fit to print, plus extensive newspapers, magazines, videos, etc.; **The Tiki Ti**: a great little hole-in-the-wall, usually real crowded, featuring big blue drinks, parasols, Martin Denny music, waterfalls and petrified blowfish - it looks like the Cramps decorated this place, and the amount of rum in the drinks makes 'em positively psychedelic! **Le Bar Cito** is a Hispanic gay disco with occasional drag shows, and close by is **Rough Trade**, which advertises "sex, leather and spurs". Also, occurring around the third weekend in August is the **Sunset Junction Street Fair**, a neighborhood must with carnival rides, games, massage and henna booths, ethnic dance groups, and tons of live bands - everyone from L7 to X, Dave Alvin, Wanda Jackson, you name it - have played here for free. A totally fun three-day event where you literally bump into everyone you know. Way fun!

THE WESTSIDE: VENICE, SANTA MONICA, BRENTWOOD & WEST LA
Aida Cynthia DeSantis (aka Cindy Pop)

There are a gazillion places and things to do on the Westside. There are the usual tourist sensations like the Strand in Venice. I have friends who come to visit and this is the first place they want to go. They want to go see **Muscle Beach** because it's been in so many movies. There's entertainment on every corner: dancers, chainsaw jugglers, balloon clowns, musicians, singers, street vendors, shops, cheap incense and sage anywhere, hair braiding, face painting, mendhi for your arms, hang on the beach, rent a bike, rent skates, go boogie boarding, make new friends, join a cult, buy a new pair of rose-colored sunglasses, forget your troubles, float around and be somebody else for the day. The Santa Monica Pier is worth the trip, it has one of the most beautiful carousels ever, an arcade and a giant Ferris wheel.

Another fun crowded place to waste a day is the **Third Street Promenade** in Santa Monica. It has stores, restaurants and movie houses galore. **Santa Monica Place** (310-394-1049), a cool mall as far as malls go, sits at the beginning of the Promenade. A nice variety of stores, they have a **Hot Topic** which is the latest rave and **K B Toys**. Toy stores are a pleasurable habit of mine, **Puzzle Zoo** (1413 3rd St. Promenade, 310-393-9201) is top grade but pricey unless you catch a sale. They have a great selection of stuffed animals. There are those days though you must buy some new particular toy that will be out of stock everywhere, this is the place you will find it. **Hennessey & Ingalls Art & Architecture Books** (1254 3rd St. Promenade, 310-458-9074) is great for browsing and drooling. Spend an afternoon there reading and they won't bother you to leave. Nearby is **Midnight Special** bookstore (1318 3rd Street Promenade, 310-393-2923); they have booksignings, poetry readings and lots of cool cultural stuff of political and social importance in a nice spacious back room. I have gotten to meet some of the coolest people there. Both these bookstores were there long before all the big cappuccino fancies book palaces opened all over the Westside. I must confess though, **Rizzoli** bookstore (332 Santa Monica Blvd., 310-393-0101) has beautiful books that I've never seen anywhere else. When the Promenade is crowded it's fun to grab a seat on a bench by one of the giant dinosaur topiaries (one of the best public art projects ever, conceptual, functional and dinosaurs all at the same time, how cool is that?) and just people-watch; you don't need to spend any money and it's fun to do with friends or by your lonesome.

This is a chance for me to segue to music, my favorite subject; there is a lot of cool Westside stuff retailwise. There's **Pyramid Music** (1340 3rd St. Promenade, 310-393-5877), which carries a nice wide variety of musical selections. The overall best music-recycling place in Santa Monica is **Record Surplus** (11609 Pico Blvd., West LA, 310-478-4217), although when selling stuff it is very easy to end up spending the money right there. Nearby is one of the best sheet music and book stores in the world, **Musician's Supply Shop** (11732 West Pico Blvd., West LA, 310-478-7836) has everything musical ever printed and if they don't, they can find it. A lot of friends into vinyl speak highly of the **House of Records** (3328 Pico Blvd., 310-450-1222) which special orders also. Another great independent record store that buys your used stuff and has a great collection of '70s and '80s music and imports is **Benway Records** (1600 Pacific Ave., Venice, 310-396-8898) in Venice. The storeowners are really sweet and love to talk music. I never go into scary Westwood but **Rhino Records** has a BLOWOUT Outlet Store (1720 Westwood Blvd., Westwood, 310-474-3786), nothing in the place is over $4.99, it's a day trip worth planning. If you are looking to buy a guitar or bass, one of the best places with a sweet selection is **Truetone Music** (714 Santa Monica Blvd., 310-393-8232).

There are a lot of movie theaters on the Westside. **Laemmle's Monica 4** (1332 2nd St., S.M., 310-394-9741) offers foreign and obscure movies you won't find at the other houses. Other worthwhile movie houses are the cheap (cheap is good!) **Aero** (1328 Montana Ave., S.M., 310-395-4990), **Nuwilshire** (1314 Wilshire Blvd., S.M., 310-394-8099) where I saw *Hedwig* 10 times while it was there, and of course the wonderful Queen of Art movie houses, the **Nuart** (11272 Santa Monica Blvd., LA, 310-478-6379) which still runs midnight shows of *Rocky Horror*, can you believe it?

There's not a lot but there are some Westside bars that offer good live original music. **Liquid Kitty** (11780 W. Pico Blvd., W. LA, 310-473-3707) is the best cocktail lounge ever.

Music happens throughout the week, try the house special vodka and horseradish martini, just for the experience. The **Temple Bar** (1026 Wilshire Blvd., S.M., 310-393-6611) is one of the hippest newest clubs on the Westside. A beautiful club with great food, a great stage and sound system all for a reasonable cover charge. It is known mostly for featuring world beat, Latin, Afro-Cuban and hip hop but they have a creative booker that gives stage time to a wide variety of music. Some cool indie acts have played in a little rock and roll dive bar called **14 Below** (1348 14th St., S.M., 310-451-5040). They also have a lot of tribute bands (Zep, the Dead, Yes, Genesis… you get the picture), which you know sometimes on the right natural high with a tacky light show can be a hell of a lot of fun. **Topper's Restaurant** (the top floor of the Radisson Huntley Hotel, 2nd and Wilshire Blvd., S.M., 310-393-8080) has acoustic music Wednesday through Saturday nights. This place also has the best view of the ocean and the best happy hour food you will find on the Westside. A favorite secret place that features classy jazz music nightly is the **Round Table Restaurant** (2460 Wilshire Blvd., S.M., 310-828-2217). **Harvelle's** (1432 4th St., S.M., 310-395-1676) is a great old blues club, a lot of older acts but they keep it fresh with a lot of new acts too, music nightly with a small cover charge. A couple of coffeehouses that have open mics, poetry, and music during the week are the **Un-Urban Coffeehouse** (3301 Pico Blvd., S.M., 310-315-0056) and **Anastasia's Asylum** (1028 Wilshire Blvd., S.M., 310-394-7113).

Santa Monica holds a lot of free festivals throughout the year featuring live music and performances. The **Clover Park Festival** at Clover Park and the **Italia Festival** on the Promenade are a few examples. There are many, call the Santa Monica Convention and Visitors Bureau (310-319-6263) for a schedule. The International Society for Krishna Consciousness

(310-836-2676) turns Venice and Santa Monica Beach into a wonderful happy Shangri-la every summer called the **Festival of Chariots**. Parades of four-story high flowered floats walk down the boardwalk. Free vegetarian food and a peek at Krishna culture with booths and art displays are offered to the public. It's a day full of thousands of happy dancing people. The Santa Monica Pier (310-458-8900) **Twilight Dance Series** offers free summer concerts on Thursday nights with fantastic, eclectic, world-renowned bands, very crowded but some of the best live music you will ever hear for absolutely no charge.

If you have a little money and want to see a live music show, on the top of my list is (of all places) a music store, **McCabe's Guitar Shop** (3101 Pico Blvd., S.M., 310-828-4497). Allen Ginsberg and Jim Carroll were two of my faves there; all the cool kings and queens of folk have performed at this kicked-back venue. They move the guitar displays in a large back room and make a concert hall with folding chairs. The stage's staircase allows the artists to climb down from the green room. What a classic entrance.

Theaters are fun but can cost money. Most places usually have a volunteer job that you can do for that evening's entrance fee, call ahead and ask. I have thrown out trash, ushered, ripped tickets, and swept many a place to see a show. The **Odyssey Theater** (2055 S. Sepulveda Blvd., W. LA, 310-477-2055) stages some really good off-the-wall quirky plays. For performance art, my heart belongs to **Highways Performance Space** (1651 18th St., 18th Street Arts Complex, S.M., 310-453-1755). I have seen Phranc, Karen Finley, Tim Miller, Annie Sprinkle, Ron Athey, Lypsinka, the late great Quentin Crisp and so many others perform here. Highways is a safe place with a wonderful soul and a 110-seat capacity that offers a venue to voices that would not usually have a chance to be heard anywhere. It was happening and being supportive long before being "out" or different was cool and I have spent some of the best nights of my life nestled in the warm glow of its house lights. They also offer workshops. Call, get a calendar, VOLUNTEER. Another cool alternative venue I have started to spend more time at is **The Electric Lodge** (1416 Electric Ave., Venice, 310-306-1854), another small theater that presents new works and has some of the funnest workshops to be found anywhere from singing to learning the history of gypsy dances.

Some of the best poetry readings happen at **Beyond Baroque Literary Arts Center** (681 Venice Blvd., Venice, 310-822-3006). Check out its extremely well-stocked bookstore, which features a lot of works by local writers. Beyond Baroque is located next door to **Social and Public Arts Resource Center** (685 Venice Blvd., Venice, 310-822-9560), affectionately known as **SPARC**. These neighbors are two of the coolest places on earth. Check out the murals and public art that comes out of SPARC. These places are non-profit arts organizations and can always use volunteers. Call them up, get a schedule, volunteering at a non-profit is an exchange you will find rewarding and you get to meet people that really care about the arts. **Dutton's Brentwood Books** (11975 San Vicente Blvd., Brentwood, 310-476-6263) always offers great readings by some of the crème of the coolest literary stars. This stretched-out store is so full of books you can get lost for hours.

Art is everywhere, whether you want it or not. The Westside loves public art. There's that gigantic weather aged **Borofsky Ballerina Clown** at Main and Rose in Venice (can you see me rolling my eyes?). Some of my favorite alternative or artist-run art places are **The Artists' Gallery** (nickname: **TAG**, 2903 Santa Monica Blvd., S.M., 310-829-9556) and the new gallery **Cherrydelosreyes** (13611 Venice Blvd., Mar Vista, 310-398-7404). **The 18th Street Arts Complex** (1639 18th St., S.M.,

310-453-3711) also warrants a mention, it is a little acre tucked away in the ever-growing music and movie industrialization that is taking over the Westside. This little piece of art heaven is full of artists and arts organizations of all mediums and disciplines and always has a lot of activities happening. They put out a calendar, call them. A couple of cool galleries located in the complex are the very alternative **Highways Gallery** (in the lobby of Highways Performance Space, 1651 18th Street, S.M., 323-666-7993), and **Crazy Space** (1629 18th St., Studio 2, S.M., 310-829-9789) run by a group of artists who are reawakening a new genre of some of the best interactive live art conceived in a long time. There are the conglomerate projects like the art mall **Bergamot Station** (2525 Michigan Blvd., at Olympic Blvd., S.M., 310-829-5854) where you can stumble into a bunch of galleries all at once. A few of my favorites: Tom Patchett's **Track 16 Gallery** (310-264-4678); **Patricia Correia Gallery** (310-264-1760); **The Gallery of Functional Art** (310-829-6990); **Robert Berman Gallery** (310-315-9506); **Shoshana Wayne Gallery** (310-453-7535); and **BGH Gallery** (310-315-9502). The Bergamot schedules all their openings on the same night and you can get totally buzzed and satiated on food, drink, art, and artspeak by the end of the evening. Don't miss them! There are galleries all over the Westside worth checking out; **FIG** (2419 Michigan Ave., S.M., 310-829-0345); **Blum and Poe** (2042 Broadway, S.M., 310-453-8311); **Christopher Grimes Gallery** (916 Colorado Blvd., S.M., 310-587-3373); and **G. Ray Hawkins Gallery** (908 Colorado Blvd., S.M., 310-394-5558) are all located in Santa Monica. There are some good ones in Venice; **La Louvre** (45 N. Venice Blvd., 310-822-4955); **Griffin Contemporary**; the **Sponto Gallery** (7 Dudley Ave., 310-399-2078); and the **William Turner Gallery** (77 Market St., 310-392-8399). There's the quirky **California Heritage Museum** (2612 Main St., S.M.,

310-392-8537), with its great collections and cheap admission. The museum that tops them all though is the **Museum of Jurassic Technology** (9341 Venice Blvd., W. LA, 310-836-6131), the weirdest, funniest, most offbeat time you can have anywhere.

Gather some friends for a picnic in a park, some let you bring your dog on the grounds; **Reed Park** (Lincoln and Wilshire, S.M., 310-458-8540) has tennis courts; **Memorial Park** (14th and Olympic, S.M., 310-450-1121); **Clover Park** (2700 Ocean Park Blvd., S.M., 310-450-4436); and **Virginia Avenue Park** (3200 Virginia Ave., S.M., 310-458-8688) are great places to spend afternoons with friends and families. Picnic tables are also found all along the coast, and if you go up Pacific Coast Highway past Point Dume there are campgrounds - perfect for a weekend I've-got-to- get-away-now break.

Anywhere you can get a cheap filling meal under $10 is alright by me. My favorites by genre are; **House of Teriyaki** (nickname: **HOT**, 1715 Pacific Ave., Venice, 310-396-9938), where me and my friends eat the most, great simple home food right next to the beach; the **Apple Pan** (10801 W. Pico Blvd., Westwood, 310-475-3585): sit at the counter for a hickory burger and a piece of banana cream pie; **Aunt Kizzy's Back Porch** (Villa Marina Shopping Center, 4325 Glencoe Ave., Marina Del Rey, 310-578-1005) for the best soul food and barbecue in the area; **The Spitfire Grill** (3300 Airport Ave., S.M., 310-397-3455) offers basic fare in a charming setting where you can sit eating breakfast outside in the nice weather as small planes take off and land at the Santa Monica Airport; **Versailles Restaurant** (10319 Venice Blvd., LA, 310-558-3168), serving Cuban food extraordinaire, get the Cuban-style pork and *arroz con pollo*; and **Fritto Misto** (601 Colorado Blvd., S.M., 310-458-2829) for good-size servings of Italian pasta and Greens and Gorgonzola, a house specialty salad; **Toi** on Wilshire

(1120 Wilshire Blvd., S.M., 310-394-7804) for "Rockin' Thai Food" you can enjoy daily until 3 a.m. surrounded by someone's collection of great rock and roll memorabilia: and for Mexican, also open until 3 a.m. (that's a good thing for Undergrounders; **La Cabana Restaurant** (738 Rose Ave., Venice, 310-392-7973) for Margaritas in a wild assortment of flavors to go along with your flan.

Drive the Pacific Coast Highway along the coastline with its eternal spiritual beach. Explore! There are tons of great window-shopping opportunities on Abbot Kinney Blvd. in Venice, which also has a neighborhood street fair every year. Santa Monica's Main Street is fun to investigate, with fun stores like **Ritual Adornments** (2708 Main St., S.M., 310-452-4044) where you can buy that one special bead to make the necklace of your dreams; **Clouds** (2719 Main St., S.M., 310-399-2059), a fun gift shop; and the **Novel Cafe** (212 Pier Ave., S.M., 310-396-8566), lined with brimming bookshelves - readables available for cheap purchase or just to browse while drinking your java. Venice Boulevard between Centinela Blvd. and Grandview is home to wild fun wacky places like **Robinson's Beautilities** (12320 Venice Blvd., M.V., 310-398-5757) for when you are in the mood for trying on wigs; the **Mad Hatter** (12306 Venice Blvd., M.V., 310-397-5777) is a party and costume shop; a bunch of thrift shops with vintage stuff right in a row; **Dick's True Value Hardware Store** (12216 Venice Blvd., M.V., 310-397-3220) where they make keys for an unbelievable 33 cents each; **Record Rover** (12204 Venice Blvd, M.V., 310-390-3132), a record store with a great selection of 45's; and **Tabu Tattoo** (12206 Venice Blvd., M.V., 310-391-5181), run by Dottie M. and R.J. Tell them Cindy sent you (please note this does not get you a discount). It's the cleanest, friendliest, neatest decorated (by R.J. himself) tattoo shop; they have one of the best piercers there, too.

TO LOS ANGELES

Two new stores have recently opened up on the Westside that are worth checking out. **Brat** (1938 14th St., S.M., 310-452-2480; www.bratstore.com) is a somewhat glam rock and roll clothing and shoe store, which in this day and age is nothing new, but what makes this store important is Nancy, the store owner. She sends out sweet weekly emails that tell you what she has in the store for purchase that week but also what is happening around town, cool new bands, djs, new clubs, causes worth supporting, stuff to do. It just seems like she knows everything and everybody. The other cool new store is **Giant Robot** (2015 Sawtelle Blvd., West LA, 310-478-1819, www.giantrobot.com), run by the same people who publish *Giant Robot*, an Asian Pop journal. This store is unbelievable and has stuff you can not get anywhere else. It's a glimpse into another world that can be breathtaking sometimes just for its sheer and simple kitschiness. It is the kind of store that you could walk into depressed and walk out smiling and happy.

There are a few places where I really like to go when the world is crazy and I need a moment to regroup and don't you need that in LA, even on the Westside; The pretty Madonna (no, not that one, the original one!) shrine outside **St. Anne's Catholic Church** (2017 Colorado Blvd., S.M., 310-829-4411); the ocean (you know where it is!); and **Woodlawn Cemetery** (1847 14th St., S.M., 310-450-0781). Back east where I come from, every little town had an aging graveyard, the ones with the broken and giant headstones, not the new graveyards with the little flat plaques that don't let you put anything next to the stone. The graveyards I'm talking about are the ones that were beautiful altars that screamed to the world you were here: flowers, pictures, spinning pinwheels and balloons scattered all over the grounds. All of my friends and I would gather there at night and pick a grave marker. We would hold hands and sit around making up fabulous or tumultuous stories of that person's life, somehow hoping the dead would join in and say yeah or no this was the way it went down. This graveyard takes me to those memories in an instant. I have been to all the bigger ones all over LA and the Valley, but this one is as perfect and comforting as the ones back home.

TRIPPING THROUGH LAUREL CANYON
(Not that kind of tripping)
Decadent Lifestyles of the Rich, Famous and (for the most part) Dead
Libby Molyneaux and Joe Hill

Only a few minutes from the Sunset Strip is **Laurel Canyon**, the famous refuge favored more by boho musicians, writers and porn stars than the glamorous set who flock to the ritzier canyons to the west. Today, it's home to a gaggle of sitcom actors who drive Ford Explorers, but not so long ago Laurel Canyon was like a freaky Shangri-La. This is an LA history tour tailored to people who, with just a bit of imagination, want to peek in and imagine what inspired Joni Mitchell, Jim Morrison, and John Holmes to call it home. While many of the sights are part of popular LA lore, elements of its wild past can still be discovered with a little sniffing. And a lot of sniffing has gone on in Laurel Canyon.

The following route was designed to be explored by bicycle. Or you can walk it in sections. Few souls are seen peddling around here, so you may even get cheers of encouragement from neighbors. (And who knows, maybe Ice-T, who lives up here, will invite you in for a glass of his eponymous beverage.) Yes, parts of it are excruciatingly steep and evil, but not only will you be rewarded with some of the most stupendous views of LA (some of which are not accessible by car), but you can feel just like Pamela and Jim as you trudge the hilly terrain, smell the eucalyptus and get the same dizzy sensation on the majestic overlooks. (If you must drive, at least listen to some John Mayall/Doors tapes, and stop and get out as much as possible.)

1. A good starting point is the **Canyon Country Store** (2108 Laurel Canyon Blvd.), with its flowery sign still dayglo-ing. Harry Houdini, who had quite a spread up the street, never bought a six-pack here, but you can usually count on seeing some luminary stocking up on better-quality munchies.

2. That's **Jim Morrison's house** (now rebuilt) on Rothdell Trail, next to the cleaners. Rumor has it he may have done a drug in these parts.

3. View time! Head up (and up and up) Kirkwood Drive. At the top, take a very sharp left on Grand View Drive (level ground!) then take a quick, very sharp right on **Colecrest Drive**. It's steep again for a bit; then turn right to stay on Colecrest and it's a very steep 50 feet until you have a 270-degree view that sweeps Laurel Canyon, all the way to the familiar sights of Hollywood and downtown, including the Griffith Park Observatory, the Hollywood sign, and the Capitol Records Building. It's a knockout.

4. Continue to the top of Colecrest Drive (you're almost there already). You'll pass over a driveway to get to Blue Heights Drive; look down and through the bushes to see the Big Blue Whale, a.k.a. the Pacific Design Center, while going downhill. Blue Heights spits you out on Sunset Plaza Drive: turn right, after a gradual uphill and a few twists it turns into Appian Way. Take a break at the **former home of Carole King** (8815 Appian Way). In the late '60s, she sat in the house's bay window for the cover of *Tapestry*.

5. Next, fly down Lookout (look out!) Mountain Avenue. (It's dangerous and skinny - did we mention bicyclists should wear a helmet?) Turn left at Wonderland Elementary School (uphill again!). It's a steep climb - **Alice Cooper**, **Keith Moon**, **John Densmore**, **David Crosby**, and **John Mayall** lived on this street. At the top, it bends right, then left, and turns into a dirt road. It makes a loop, full of ruts - but at least it's flat! This secret (until now) gem of a view boasts incredible (and incredibly quiet) southward views of Beverly Hills to the ocean (and Catalina when the fog tide is low). As an added bonus, you can peek down into people's backyards and swimming pools and see straight down Doheny.

6. Now descend back down Wonderland Avenue. Well-endowed porn star **John Holmes** was accused (and acquitted) of murdering five people in a drug-related incident at 8763 Wonderland Avenue in '81.

7. Take a sharp left and go up Wonderland Park Avenue. Right on Greenvalley Road; left on Crest View Drive; left on Skyline Drive to Mulholland Drive and head right (east). Try to pick out the house on Mulholland where **Danny Sugarman**, former Doors associate who co-wrote *No One Here Gets Out Alive*, flew his car off the road and onto a house, after a night of alcohol and Quaaludes at the Rainbow Room on the Strip. The car landed right side up on the flat roof of somebody's

house, caving it in; Danny and his girlfriend left the car in the living room and walked to his house on Wonderland to do speedballs. Happily (and surprisingly), Danny's still alive.

8. Continue on Mulholland through the light at Laurel Canyon Boulevard. Almost immediately, make a right on Woodrow Wilson Drive. This shady, mostly flat bucolic road has more than its share of grisly history. At 8000 Woodrow Wilson, actress **Inger Stevens** overdosed in 1970 at age 35 (she played Katy on mid-'60s sitcom *The Farmer's Daughter*). At 7944, another little-known starlet **Gia Scala** drank and pilled herself to death in 1972 at age 38. And nearby at 7357, another Hollywood dreamer you've probably never heard of, **Aleta Alexander**, took a rifle to herself. At the age of 28, she was having trouble getting roles and had found out her more successful husband, actor **Ross Alexander**, was cheating on her. He did the same with that very rifle about a year later. 6969 is the address where character actor **Frank Christi** was shot in a drug-ambush in his carport.

9. Double back a little on Woodrow Wilson and turn right (north) on Passmore Drive; right on Oakshire Drive; and left on Oak Glen Drive. At 3429 Oak Glen is the house where Oakland Raider/actor **John Matusak** croaked after drugs attacked his heart in 1989.

10. Enough death already. Wind back to Woodrow Wilson, go right (west) a little and turn left on Montcalm (south) and left on Pyramid Place to get to Mulholland. Across the street is the entrance to Runyon Canyon. Take the dirt path up and down to one of the many lookout spots where you have the City of Angels at your feet. If it's a smoggy day, you can just make out an **Angelyne** billboard a little west of the Capitol Records building. There's something special about being in this untamed, wild park knowing that you're 1,200 feet above an entirely different sort of untamed, wild place.

TO LOS ANGELES

11. Head back (west) on Mulholland. Turn left on Woodrow Wilson, then left (south) on Woodstock Road, and right on Willow Glen Road, which takes you down to Laurel Canyon Boulevard. On the southeast corner are the sprawling remains of the **Harry Houdini** estate. It was only the widow Houdini who actually called the rambling hillside manor home, but her Halloween séances to bring back Harry's spirit are legendary. After a devastating fire, the only structural remains are the stone fireplaces and staircases, along with a dilapidated servant's quarters. We recommend you keep your distance at night - creepy crawlies of the human persuasion are regularly seen coming and going. During the day, it's easy to connect the dots and imagine the elegant parties in the early 1900s. The vacant lot at Lookout Mountain and Laurel Canyon Boulevard is where **Frank Zappa** lived from '66-'68. Just up at 2451 Laurel Canyon Boulevard is the haunted mansion where the **Red Hot Chili Peppers** recorded *Bloodsugarsexmagic*. Members of **Love and Rockets** lived here until a fire damaged the inside in '96.

12. Go up Lookout Mountain a little. Below Wonderland Avenue Elementary School is **Joni Mitchell**'s former home where she lived during her *Ladies of the Canyon* and "Clouds" period. Picture Joni looking out the kitchen window and sketching the cover drawing for *Ladies of the Canyon*. Her live-in lover at the time, Graham Nash, wrote "Our House" about this very, very, very fine house. Do not disturb the two cats in the yard.

P.S. Remember: The Thomas Bros. are an LA explorer's best friends. Get one of their guides before launching on this worthwhile expedition. For further reading, check out *Wonderland Avenue* by Danny Sugarman; Ken Schessler's *This Is Hollywood* and *The LA Musical History Tour* by Art Fein.

PASADENA AND BEYOND
Mary Herczog

Way up here in the real hills, in the other Valley (San Gabriel, thank you very much), we, the residents of Altadena and Pasadena, have to constantly explain to the geographically-impaired that we are not off the face of the earth. Actually, we are a mere twenty minutes away from Hollywood, by freeway. And frankly, everything in Los Angeles is at least twenty minutes away from everything else, not to mention freeway accessible. Here you can get away from some of the crowds, see much more of the truly lovely architecture that originally characterized LA (but in most of the rest of the city has been torn down in favor of mini-malls), gawk at the mountains, and even walk around ...a rare occurrence in most of the greater Los Angeles area.

TO LOS ANGELES

ALTADENA

Since it's neither a city nor a neighborhood of a city, Altadena suffers from a serious identity crisis. But check this out; the North Hollywood bank robbers (the Kevlar-clad, Uzi-toting guys who went down in a haze of bullets and glory in early 1997) were Altadena residents, as was motorist Rodney King. We don't have crime - we just export it to other parts of the city. But we do have Jackie Robinson's alma mater. Yes, the first black major league ballplayer went to **Muir High School** (1905 Lincoln Ave.).

Drive north on Lincoln into the hills area called the La Vina development. This was the site of the La Vina Sanitarium. In 1931, Winnie Ruth Judd was picked up for questioning after someone noticed the trunk she had with her on the train to LA smelled - it was full of hacked up bodies (those of her ex-room-mates). Winnie escaped from police questioning and walked twenty miles to hide out at the sanitarium (where she had once been a patient) before giving herself up.

Go back down Lincoln to Altadena Dr. and turn left (heading east). As the houses get nicer, you might suddenly think you are in Beverly Hills - particularly if you watch *Beverly Hills, 90210*. You'd be right; much of the show's exteriors are filmed here and in Pasadena. That's Brandon and Brenda Walsh's house on the left, at 1675.

Do bananas mean more to you than just fruit or phallic symbols? Then get right over the **Banana Museum** (2524 N. El Molino, 1-900-Bananas, usually open by appointment only), a shrine to all things banana. More things banana than you ever dreamed possible.

If you feel like a hike, drive up to **Cheney Trail** (off Loma Alta, between Lincoln and Fair Oaks). Park at the top, and hike down to the waterfall or campgrounds. You can also try **Eaton Canyon**, just off Altadena Dr. to the west. For those who prefer to take their exercise in a different way, have a stroll in the **Mountain View Cemetery** (2400 N. Fair Oaks Ave., 626-794-7133). Thanks to the dreaded Hubert Eaton (the man who brought us Forest Lawn and the modern concept of "memorial parks" with those flat, flush-to-the-ground headstones), cemeteries, particularly out here (where Eaton flourished) have lost a lot of their ambiance. Mountain View still has plenty of upright headstones, which are growing very rare. Consequently, even with the palm trees, this is everything a good, eerie cemetery should be - with a little extra Raymond Chandler atmosphere.

FOOD AND DRINK

Fox's (2352 N. Lake, 626-797-9430): A tiny hole-in-the-wall local tradition with a coffeehouse (serving some fine iced mochas) in the back. Expect long weekend breakfast lines - their biscuits and cream gravy is to die for. Check out the scary stuffed foxes on the walls.

Dutch Oven Bakery (2281 N. Lake, 626-794-3555): Friendly, family-run business with huge tasty muffins, cake made from scratch, and fresh bread. The owner often waits on customers and everyone who works here will chat about everything from computers to Bill Clinton's sex life.

Aunt Gussye's Place (2057 N. Los Robles, 626-794-6024): Authentic New Orleans food, from red beans and rice to shrimp in a buttery, garlic sauce, to fried fish po'boys. Okay, it's not as good as you would get in Louisiana, but if you need a fix, it does the trick.

Taste of New Orleans (2545 N. Fair Oaks, 626-791-6879): Altadena's legendary Burnette's BBQ closed and everyone has been in mourning. But this place is doing its best to take over. Ask them to make things hot and check out the fish.

Patticakes (1900 N. Allen, 626-794-1120): An expensive

chi-chi bakery, but with high-rent muffins and pastries to die for. Go ahead - blow your budget.

Little **Middle Eastern** places, from cafes to grocery stores, are found if you drive around on both Allen (south of Patticakes), and east and west on Washington (using Allen as the center). Each is totally different and worth taste testing. (The grocerystore on Allen is particularly fun; try the fresh meat and cheese-topped breads they have delivered every morning.)

STORES

Mitchell Books (1394 E. Washington Blvd., 626-798-4438): Run by a massive, tattooed biker-type guy who is as liberal and left wing as it gets, Mitchell Books has every crime/mystery novel you can think of - and many you didn't know existed. The owner is incredibly chatty; he talks knowledgeably about politics (on both a global and local scale) and just about anything else you can imagine. He also makes trustworthy book recommendations - he knows his stuff.

PASADENA

Best known for floral floats and perfect-appearing weather on New Year's Day, Pasadena is usually hidden the rest of the time - because originally, it was Old Money, and that's the way Old Money likes it. It's becoming more high profile of late, thanks to a renovation of **Old Town Pasadena**, the stretch of Colorado Blvd. usually seen as part of The Parade. (Don't forget the anti-Rose Parade, the **Doo-Dah Parade**, which takes place Thanksgiving Day weekend, and features such entries as the Synchronized Briefcase Drill Team. It's an ode to the eccentric.) The crumbling 1920s office buildings had fallen into slum-like disrepair, and a few years ago quite a lot of money was sunk into renovating and cleaning up the place. Unfortunately, upscale chain stores (Gap, J. Crew, Victoria's Secret) came in, pushing out most of the mom-and-pop independent stores and turning the place into a (very pretty) outdoor mall. And attracting crowds; if you really like the concept of personal space, skip this area on a Friday or Saturday night. However, it is a nice place to hang out on an uncrowded night. (The **AMC** offers "twilight shows"; any movie showing between 4 and 6 p.m. is $3.75, which is darn near affordable.) Plus, the **Adult Bookstore** is still holding their ground; bless their hearts, they took their grimy, trench coat-like exterior and redid it in yuppie glass and neon to blend in with their newly upscale neighbors. Around the corner, also resisting extinction by yuppification, is a **botanica** with some truly scary items - check out the Sacred Garlic candles! Every kitchen needs one.

On Fair Oaks, just south of Green (which is parallel to Colorado, on the south), look up at the side of the building on the west and read these words: "Lawrence, picking up his fork." Originally, it read, " 'My people are the people of the desert,' said T. E. Lawrence, picking up his fork." The Whittier earthquake badly damaged this old building, and some bricks with most of the words fell off, so it started at "said T. E. Lawrence" for many years. Recently, a paint job obscured even more of it, further increasing its cryptic nature.

The **Castle Green Hotel** is a residence hotel that covers nearly a block between Raymond and Fair Oaks, on Green St. It's a gorgeous, huge old Gothic number and one can't help but think the people who live there are very lucky. The following are other Old Town establishments worth visiting: **Equator Coffee House** (22 Mills Pl., 626-564-8656) is a funky, airy place with not only a huge variety of coffee drinks, but also some righteous smoothies (and flavored hot chocolate with flavored whip cream!). They stood in as the "gay coffeehouse" on *Beverly Hills, 90210*. Ignore the Starbucks across the street

(Equator is actually hidden in an alley off Colorado) and come to the real McCoy. *90210* buffs can also go to the **Peach Pit** (45 S. Fair Oaks), which is really **Ruby's Diner** — the exterior, then the venerable Rose City Cafe — was used in the show.)

Old Town Bakery (166 W. Colorado, 626-793-2993) features giant elaborate desserts, like the frosting-intensive Milky Way Cake (must be eaten to be believed), enormous scones and so forth. Many other restaurants in LA serve desserts made here. Please ask them to bring back the Zebra Cake (white and milk chocolate mousse surrounded by white and chocolate checkerboard cake); it was my favorite dessert and I've never recovered from its loss. They also have regular food, most of it pretty healthy; quiches, big salads, sandwiches on there own fabulous bread. Very crowded for brunch on Sundays. Has a pretty outdoor patio.

Kuala Lampur (132 W. Colorado Blvd., 626-577-5175) may be your only chance to try Malaysian food - outside of Malaysia, that is. Think Thai, only different.

Merida (20 E. Colorado Blvd., 626-792-7371) serves Yucatan food; located (more or less) between Mexico proper and Cuba - and so is the food. Highly tasty.

Rebecca's Dream (16 S. Fair Oaks, 626-796-1200). Somewhat overpriced vintage store, but they will bargain things down.

Raymond News Stand (first block of Raymond south of Colorado). Openly gay and into alt. culture, with a decent stock of periodicals, gay/lesbian, and alternative reading matter; the stock isn't what it used to be but it's much better than offered elsewhere in Pasadena.

Hot Hot Hot (130 N. Fair Oaks at CJ's Gourmet) Hot sauces, hot peppers, hot oils — really, anything that can be made with chilies. Out You Devil hot sauce, Vampire's Kiss hot sauce, all kinds of sauces you never knew about but burn the roof of your mouth. Some of the labels on the sauces are so hilarious, you don't care if they taste good.

Soda Jerks (219 S. Fair Oaks, 626-583-8031) is actually just a little south of Old Town, but is an airy, old-fashioned-looking (maybe with genuine fixtures) soda fountain, that serves the fabulous Fosselman's ice cream. Not as good as Fair Oaks Soda Fountain in S. Pasadena, and a little more expensive, but much much better than going to a prefab place. They also serve food.

FLEA MARKETS

Pasadena is home to the two best flea markets in Southern California. The first is at **Pasadena City College** (1570 E. Colorado Blvd.). Free on the first Sunday of the month. It's a good size; big, but not so big you can't cover the whole ground. Record nerds will find nirvana (or Nirvana) at the Record Swap portion, where vinyl still rules. The Aes-Nihil gang (including former Germs drummer Don Bolles) can often be found holding court in this section, and selling serial killer, Manson-related, Church of Satan, and other underground pop culture books, along with their massive collection of naughty/subversive videos (we recommend the infamous Go-Go's porno tape). The second Sunday of the month hosts the mammoth **Rose Bowl Swap Meet** (1001 Rose Bowl Dr.). It's the mother of all swap meets, covering acres of ground, including genuine antique dealers, piles of junk, and new tacky items; just when you think you've seen it all you find another football field full of stuff. There is an admission fee (up to $10; early birds get a discount, not to mention the best pickings).

MUSEUMS

No mention of Pasadena can neglect the **Norton Simon Museum** (411 W. Colorado Blvd., 626-449-6840), a world-

class collection mostly devoted to Impressionists and their con-
temporaries. But far cooler is the **Huntington Library Art
Collections and Botanical Gardens** (1151 Oxford Rd., San
Marino, 626-405-2141). Formerly the vast estate of a robber
baron, like the Getty family after him, he turned his art collection and home into a museum. The grounds are huge and varied;
one moment you are walking on English estate type grounds,
complete with rolling lawns, large trees and the odd sculpture;
the next minute you are in a tropical jungle, or a desert filled
with cactus and other succulents. There's a Japanese garden
with a teahouse, babbling brook and Half Moon Bridge. There's
a rose garden. A Shakespeare garden. And on (and on) it goes.
The library itself has a Guttenberg Bible on display, among
many other treasures. And the art museum, housed in
Huntington's own former residence, has still more fabulous
items, including Gainsborough's *Blue Boy* and the matching
painting known as *Pinky*. Pay them a visit, but once you've
marveled at their icon status, look at the same wall *Blue Boy* is
on, all the way to the right. See the painting of a dark-haired
girl in the large hat; chin perched in hand, looking coyly at
you? She's the famous Emma Hamilton, for whom British
Naval hero Lord Nelson endured so much scandal (they were
both married at the time of their lengthy affair). When you look
at this portrait, you suddenly understand what all the fuss is
about. (Now go rent *That Hamilton Woman* and see how they
superimposed Vivian Leigh's face onto a copy of this same
portrait.) Before you go to the Huntington, make a reservation
at their Rose Garden Tea Room; at around $11 for an all- you-
can eat buffet (including tasty finger sandwiches and strawber-
ries with creme fraiche): it's the best Afternoon Tea in the city.
Afterwards, you can walk off the many calories by exploring
the grounds — or just nap under a tree. (Note: there is no admission fee but they will extract a "suggested donation" from

you as you park your car.)

STORES

Vroman's Books (695 E. Colorado Blvd., 626-449-5320): Around since 1930, Vroman's is big and well-stocked. Book savvy, helpful staff. There is also a better-than-average magazine stand outside, heavy on the literary journals. And they added a cushy, mildly Victorian Gothic-looking cafe with some terrific (if pricey) desserts and some savory munchies.

Cliff's Books (630 E. Colorado, 626-449-9541) A used bookstore that is, quite honestly, a little overpriced and a bit attitudinal. But they are huge (as opposed to their two more kind-hearted and pleasant - but considerably smaller - competitors across the street; pay them a visit at the same time) and stay open until midnight every night.

Aardvark's Odd Ark (1253 E. Colorado, 626-583-9109) A chain vintage shop - they probably snatch all the good stuff from the real thrift store across the street (but just in case, go by there as well). Well-stocked, but not terribly cheap. Still, they have tons of used Levis, Army pants, racks and racks of dresses and whatnot. And they aren't nearly as rude or expensive as the branch on Melrose Avenue.

Poobah Record Shop (1101 E. Walnut. 626-449-3359) Located in an old house, in a non-business district part of Pasadena, this place is crammed with new and used CDs, some vinyl, imports and a staff that breathes music.

RESTAURANTS

Burger Continental (535 S. Lake Ave., 626-792-6634) Now wait; this is not, repeat, not a burger joint. In fact, the worst thing anyone can do is order a burger at Burger Continental. Regulars will laugh at you. You will be revealed as a tourist. Because this is one of the best Middle Eastern restaurants around. Small sums of money get you enormous plates of food. Not just the usual kebobs and shawarma, but also garlic buttery chicken, chicken stuffed with spinach and feta and pine nuts, vegetarian specialties and on and on. The menu is huger than huge, and if that's not enough, there is a whiteboard with the day's specials on it; a dozen or more combination plates, each with an adjective assuring it is "delicious!" "outstanding!" "delectable!" All dinners come with hummus, salad bar, stuffed grape leaves, and more. You will almost certainly end up with enough for lunch the next day, making the medium-priced meals even more of a bargain. Often, the owner wanders the line (you order at a window and sit in a charming patio where a band plays and a bellydancer shakes), giving discounts to everyone just for the hell of it ("First time here? Ten percent off!"). It's a wacky place and will make both veggies and carnivores happy. Go early and often.

Pie N' Burger (913 E. California Blvd., 626-795-1123) Now here, you order the burger. This is where you go when you want the real thing: big, juicy, and slathered in goopy stuff, made on a grill as you sit at a low Formica counter. Burger Heaven. The pies (and homemade cakes) aren't bad either, but skip the shakes.

Sushi of Naples (735 E. Green St., 626-578-1123) Better than average sushi - predictably fresh and tender. Call first and go only if they are still offering their Happy Hour; most of each evening they sell their sushi half-price, which makes it very affordable.

The Hat (491 N. Lake, 626-449-1844) A local food critic once made the distinction between good pastrami and bad pastrami: the former is the hearty stuff you get at a classic New York deli, the latter is the French dip, greasy-style kind; you can feel your arteries harden even as your taste buds dance in glee. And The Hat, everyone agrees, is the best of Bad Pastrami.

SOUTH PASADENA

It is indeed south of Pasadena and more small town in feeling. David Lynch staple Jack Nance (star of *Eraserhead*) got into a fight at the Winchell's Donuts at 438 Fair Oaks, and died from his injuries some days later at his home across the street at 509 Fair Oaks.

Fair Oaks Pharmacy and Soda Fountain (1526 Mission St., 818-799-1414) In operation since the '20s, but recently renovated with fixtures from a midwestern turn-of-the-century pharmacy/soda fountain; the owner's condition for sale was that it be used in a working pharmacy. So now there's a hammered tin ceiling, gorgeous wood and beveled glass cabinets, plus a marble-topped soda fountain counter. The ice cream is perfect; they use Fosselman's, a local tradition since 1913. When you taste it, you will know why. Caution: they use over a pint of ice cream in their shakes, which is more than any one person needs to consume at a sitting. Split one.

Rialto Theatre (1023 Fair Oaks, 818-799-9567) One of the last great old movie palaces, a little shabby despite some renovations. Check out the demon with red glowing eyes at the top of the proscenium. Best of all, they show art house movies: no Spielberg here. Combine this with some ice cream at the Fair Oaks Pharmacy just up the street, and you'll have a truly retro time.

The Bookhouse (1026 Fair Oaks Ave., 818-799-0756) A very well stocked used bookstore with a friendly book-aware staff, set inside a sweet Craftsman-style old house.

Senor Fish (618 Mission, 818-403-0145) Foodie and ethnic food fans know this little stand is the place to go for fish tacos.

SIERRA MADRE

This is a genuine small town plunked down in the middle

of the big city. It's got a main street lined with stores of varying interest (a great coffeshop, coupla good restaurants, a few antique stores) - and it may look oddly familiar. That's because this stood in for the small town in *Invasion of the Body Snatchers*. Wander around and feel like a pod person… just kidding. It's very pretty and peaceful. The mountains are right there with several good hiking trails; ask around for directions to the different access roads. Afterwards, have a bite at the **Corfu Cafe** (48 W. Sierra Madre Blvd., 626-355-5993). This is a good choice for a cheap breakfast or lunch; dinner is slightly more pricey but probably delicious. Service is slow, so be in the mood to dawdle. Lunch brings huge salads and sandwiches, with nothing over $6. Try the large Greek Salad, or the Brie Chicken sandwich (Brie and chicken on a French roll with bacon and red onions, all pressed down like a Cuban sandwich. It's sooo fattening. It's so delicious.)

MONTERY PARK AND ALHAMBRA

These two communities lie a bit south of South Pasadena - between ten and twenty minutes drive. If you like Chinese food, make the trip. This cannot be urged strongly enough. Forget Chinatown in downtown LA; this is the Chinese community in the LA area, and is rapidly becoming Little Hong Kong. There are dozens of Chinese restaurants down here, varying in cuisine, price, and quality. Just drive and pick one out (the huge palace-like restaurants are usually safe bets), but here are two to keep an eye out for. **Ocean Star Seafood** (112 N. Chandler Ave., Montery Park, 626-300-8446) and its larger partner around the corner on Garvey Ave. serve incredibly fresh seafood (probably caught that morning) plucked from the tank. The larger eatery also does *major* dim sum. Dumpling fans will be more than happy at **Dumpling House** (5612 Rosemead Blvd., 626-309-9918).

Fosselman's Ice Cream Parlor (1824 W. Main, Alhambra, 626-282-6533) As mentioned, this family business started making ice cream in 1913 - plenty long enough to get it oh–so-right. It's incredible stuff; you won't ever bother with Haagen-Daaz again. Several Pasadena places serve Fosselman's, but not only is it cheaper at the source, it's just fun to go to a real (if tiny) ice cream parlor again. After eating your fill of dim sum, come here and explode.

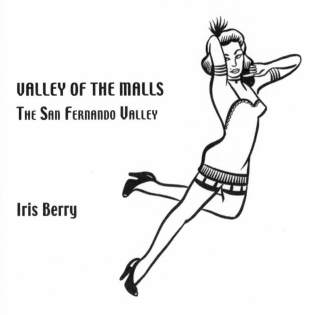

VALLEY OF THE MALLS
THE SAN FERNANDO VALLEY

Iris Berry

It doesn't matter where you are in the San Fernando Valley, if you throw a rock you're sure to hit a Mall. Being a born and raised Valley Girl, I can attest to that. Hey, I happen to love the mall, it's air-conditioned, tons of great and crappy food from all walks of life, I get great reception on my cell phone, and "like, OHMYGAWD!" there's always a sale going on. But more than malls, the San Fernando Valley has really amazing vintage stores with great prices and some truly different and unique restaurants. It's also been the setting for many historic and countercultural happenings that have reverberated throughout the world. And hey… if the Valley was good enough for Charles Manson, well then, it's good enough for me!

MALLS

GLENDALE GALLERIA (50 W. Broadway, Glendale, 818-240-9481, www.glendalegalleria.com) Rumor has it that Lux and Ivy of The Cramps have been spotted here (on more than one occasion) visiting the food court at ten in the morning. What I want to know is: what were they doing there? Make sure you take a compass with you, this place is huge.

BURBANK MALL (201 E. Magnolia Blvd., Burbank, 818-566-8617, www.mediacitycenter.com) For a little vertigo with your shopping, the Burbank Mall is known for its giant carousel. Take a ride or shop till you drop, one way or another, your money is gonna come flyin' out of your pockets. There's an **Apple Store** for your computin' needs, an awesome **Sephora** for beauty product junkies, and check out **Forever Twenty One** for bargain Britney Spears type fashions.

SHERMAN OAKS GALLERIA (15303 Ventura Blvd., Sherman Oaks, 818-382-4100, www.shermanoaksgalleria.com) Put on the map in 1982 by Moon Unit Zappa's hit song "Valley Girl." Recently remodeled, nipped, tucked and lifted… super fabulous!

FASHION SQUARE SHERMAN OAKS (14006 Riverside Dr., Sherman Oaks, 818-783-0550) The kinder, gentler mall, as I like to call it. Skylights, split level food court and convenient, stress-free roof parking. Weekends they have a piano player that takes requests. Quite the pick-up scene for the over-65 set.

NORTHRIDGE FASHION CENTER (9301 Tampa Ave., Northridge, 818-885-9700, www.northridgefashioncenter.com) Fully restored after being demolished by the '94 Northridge quake. It's back and more dazzling than ever.

WESTFIELD SHOPPINGTOWN PROMENADE (6100 Topanga Canyon Blvd., Woodland Hills, 818-884-7090, www.shoppingtown.com) Recently remodeled. High-tech theatres with those really comfy seats that move and adjust and recline (and I think if you stick a quarter in, probably vibrate). Connected to a fancy-shmancy food court.

WESTFIELD SHOPPINGTOWN TOPANGA (6600 Topanga Canyon Blvd., Canoga Park, 818-594-8740, www.shoppingtown.com) One of my first mall experiences as a child. Great food court with a real train ride in it for the young 'uns.

THE COMMONS AT CALABASAS (4799 Common Way, Calabasas, 818-222-3444) The Commons is an extremely pretty and serene outdoor mall with piped-in music and water-falls, surrounded by picturesque green rolling hills. It's a nice place to shop as long as you don't mind five-year-olds on cell phones and sixteen–year-olds driving brand new Mercedes Benz SUVs.

THE STUDIOS

NBC STUDIOS (3000 W. Alameda Ave., Burbank, 818-840-3538, www.nbc.com) NBC Studios is where the term "Beautiful Downtown Burbank" was coined during the filming of *Laugh-In*. NBC is also the place to see Jay Leno taping live. There's a 70-minute tour that takes you behind the scenes of *The Tonight Show* - wardrobe, makeup, set construction, special effects and sound effects departments. Oh boy!

WALT DISNEY STUDIOS (500 S. Buena Vista St., Burbank, 818-560-1000, www.disney.go.com) This studio offers nothing in the way of rides because it's not Disneyland; it's a *studio*, although at one time they were going to build Disneyland right across the street. Then they realized they needed more space and bought 200 acres in Anaheim instead. The studio does offer a hint of Disney in its architecture, holding up the House of Mouse are none other than the Seven Dwarves themselves. Not bad for a bunch of guys who've been around since 1937. Rumor has it that if you listen closely, you can actually hear the seven helpers whistling (while they work).

WARNER BROTHERS STUDIOS TOUR (4000 Warner Blvd., Burbank, 818-954-1744, www.seeing-stars.com/StudioTours/WarnerBrosTours.html) Offering a two-hour VIP tour that visits actual working areas and sound stages. Tours conducted by reservation only. Warner Brothers also has live tapings of shows. For tickets and information call: **Audiences Unlimited**, 818-753-3470.

UNIVERSAL STUDIOS TOUR (100 Universal City Pl., Universal City, 1-800-UNIVERSAL, www.universalstudios.com) A full day of rides, movie making, star and star-impersonator gazing, as well as Hollywood-induced earthquakes, fires, dinosaur and shark attacks. Visit old sets, too, like the *Psycho* house. Growing up with three older brothers who were constant troublemakers, this is one more place that my family almost got thrown out of. While on the set of *The Munsters* my brother Don kept trying to set Spot (the Munster's "family dragon") free. We were warned (and as usual, shamed) in front of the whole tour!

UNIVERSAL AMPHITHEATRE (100 Universal City Plaza, Universal City, 818-777-1000) a great place to see concerts, comedians and political speakers.

UNIVERSAL CITY WALK (3900 Lankershim Blvd., Universal City, 818-622-9841, www.citywalk.com) Imagine a perfect LA? City Walk has attempted to replicate all the best places in Tinsel Town and put them all in one spot. The only thing that's missing is Dodger Stadium... but I'm sure they're making plans... There's a multi-screen cinema, souvenir shops, a couple of rock clubs (with live music), good eats (both restaurants and snack stands), huge video screens, and street performers. Around Christmas they make a big outdoor ice-skating rink and rent skates. Ample parking, too.

TO LOS ANGELES

CBS STUDIOS CENTER (CBS Studio Center, 4024 Radford Ave., Studio City, 818-655-5000, www.cbs.com) One of the smaller, more homey studios... originally owned by Mack Sennett (of *Keystone Cops* fame) in the 1920s, giving the city it's name, "Studio City." Among the many TV shows that have been filmed here are *Gilligan's Island* and *Hawaii Five-O*... Now, I know the ocean shots must have been edited in, but up until the mid '80s one could actually find the Lagoon from *Gilligan's Island* in the back part of the studios. Three hour tour, my ass! They were in the Valley!

FOOD

THE CASTAWAYS (1250 Harvard Road, Burbank, 818-848-6691, www.calendarlive.com) A big banquet-type restaurant on a hill. Everywhere you sit, you get an amazing view of the San Fernando Valley and the Los Angeles skyline. Too bad the food and the service (at least in the main dining room) suck! I've tried so many times to like this place because the view is so goddamn incredible! So here's what I figured out. If you sit on the outdoor patio, around one of the fire pits with the view of the city at your feet, preferably at sundown, sip cocktails, order dinner off the moderately priced bar menu, and just stay out of the main dining room, *no matter what*, a night at the Castaways can be fabulous.

THE SMOKE HOUSE (4420 Lakeside Drive, Burbank, 818-845-3733) A Burbank staple for years, The Smoke House is conveniently located right across the street from the Warner Brothers Studios lot, and known for being a historic neighborhood hang to the stars. Also known for prime rib, painfully good garlic bread, and Sunday brunches. The Smoke House often appeared in episodes of *The Larry Sanders Show* and countless episodes of *Columbo*.

TOKYO DELVES SUSHI BAR (5239 Lankershim

Blvd., N. Hollywood, 818-766-3868, www.delve-sushibar.com) One of the wildest restaurants in town! So wild that they have a disclaimer hanging at the front door that reads, "If you stand on the chairs or the tables, we don't take responsibility or liability for anything that happens!" Loud music, fun, crazy people (including staff as well as patrons) reasonably priced sushi.

JERRY'S FAMOUS 24 HOUR DELICATESSEN (12655 Ventura Blvd., Studio City, 818-980-4245, www.jerrysdeli.com) A menu that offers over 600 dishes, including huge sandwiches, awesome kosher pickles, breakfasts, and mega-yummy fries. And no, it's not named after Jerry Seinfeld, although he is known to frequent the place so much that he even has his own table.

ZIGS "HOME OF THE BULLET" (6821 White Oak Ave., Reseda, 818-343-3679) The name pretty much explains it all! If you can't handle a Bullet? Try a "ton on a bun." Both of these burgers are smeared with grilled onions, American cheese and 1000 Island dressing on everything! Lots of good and fattening things. It's a classic neighborhood greasy spoon from another era.

EAGLES CAFE (5231 Lankershim Blvd., North Hollywood, 818-760-4212) Live punk rock, spoken word, short order food, espresso pub. It's a NoHo cornerstone. Wednesday nights feature an open mike.

DR. HOGLEY WOGLEY'S TEXAS TYLER BBQ (8136 Sepulveda Blvd., Van Nuys, 818-782-2480) For some, Dr. Hogley Wogley's is the *only* reason to come to the San Fernando Valley. Serving amazing BBQ for over 30 years.

KRISPY KREME DOUGHNUTS (7249 Van Nuys Blvd., Van Nuys, 818-908-9113, www.krispykreme.com) Doughnut heaven… or hell. It's evil enough that they give *free* hot samples and they have a 24-hour drive-up window, but to

make matters worse, they've just introduced their latest creation: the New York Cheesecake Krispy Kreme! When you
wake up from your sugar coma, contorted in your Barcalounger
in the wee hours of the morning, with the TV blaring some
strange infomercial and Krispy krumbs all over your face, and
you don't know how you got there, please, *please* don't hate
me!

SAM WOO'S BBQ (6450 North Sepulveda Blvd., Van
Nuys, 818-988-6813) Good Chinese food for less, and accord-
ing to my mom, the best war won ton soup in the Western
Hemisphere! My mother wouldn't lie!

THE QUEEN MARY (12449 Ventura Blvd., Studio City,
818-506-5619) Giving us female impersonator shows for 40
years straight... or, rather, the last forty years. The building
was originally bought from May West, go figure!

SPORTSMENS LODGE (4234 Coldwater Canyon, Studio City, 818-755-5000, www.sportsmenslodge.com) Imagine
you at the Sunday-all-you-can-eat buffet, while surrounded by
exotic gardens and a pond with real swans swimming by, trying to decide whether you want more crab legs or more lobster?
What a dilemma!

VITELLO'S (4349 Tujunga Ave., Studio City, 818-769-
0905, www.vitellos.com) Now, we all know about this place
because of a famous celebrity murder mystery - can you say
Baretta? But the food is really good, too.

AROMA CAFE (4360 Tujunga Ave., Studio City, 818-
769-3853) Great neighborhood coffeehouse and eatery.
Connected to a bookstore called "Portrait of A Bookstore" offering great books, gifts and vintage toys for kiddies. Outdoor
seating. Waterfalls, dogs and sitcom actors, oh my!

MARMALADE CAFÉ (14910 Ventura Blvd., Sherman
Oaks, 818-905-8872, www.marmaladecafe.com) This is where
you'll find porn stars, soap stars and grandmas all mingling

and eating under the same roof. Pretty country French décor (and everything you see is for sale). A great date place or a nice place to meet your mom. The food is incredible; breakfast, lunch and dinner. And the staff is extremely amiable and good looking, too.

MAZARINNO'S (12920 Riverside Dr., Sherman Oaks, 818-788-5050) The best pizza this side of New York! The interior looks like those photos of famous mob hits. Big portions and loud, just like grandma's kitchen, if grandma lived in Chicago and her last name were Capone! Their motto is "Indulge your inner Italian, everyone has one!" (Or they'll break your legs.)

COBALT CAFE (22047 Sherman Way, Canoga Park, 818-348-3789, www.cobaltcafe.com) Large, comfortable punk rock coffeehouse. Showcasing under-age hardcore bands and spoken word.

THE INN OF THE SEVENTH RAY (128 Old Topanga Canyon Rd., Topanga, 310-455-1311, www.innoftheseventhray.com) Romantic, gourmet natural food, creekside dining, no processed sugars on the premises. They've been catering to vegetarians, vegans and wheat-free eaters since the '70s. Lots of people get married here.

FOLLOW YOUR HEART (21825 Sherman Way, Canoga Park, 818-348-3240, www.followyourheart.com) Health food market and restaurant. Visiting this place is like taking a walk into the 1970s... the restaurant offers meatless clubs and Reubens. Whatever kind of diet you're on, they can cater to it.

SAGEBRUSH CANTINA (23527 Calabasas Rd., Calabasas, 818-222-6062) The Sagebrush has a reputation as being a " wild" Valley hang. Huge outdoor patio, wide screen TVs for sports events. Full bar, Mexican food, burgers, seafood, salads, and desserts. Every Sunday motorcyclists from all over meet and mix with families, tourists, strippers, and locals, becoming a regular modern day saloon and the breeding ground for the "Jewish American Biker." Big fun!

STORES

CIRCUS LIQUOR (5600 Vineland Ave., North Hollywood, 818-769-1500) This would normally be an average liquor store selling the usual items, except for the fact that it has the greatest sign in all of the Valley and Los Angeles combined, and for that matter maybe even the World! It's a 35-foot neon clown three times the size of the liquor store. Taking up most of the parking it really brightens up the otherwise dreary intersection of Burbank Blvd. and Vineland Ave. When I first discovered it in 1987, I made Pleasant (our fearless editor) take a ten-mile ride in my car, blindfolded the whole way from Hollywood, blasting, "Is That All There Is?" by Peggy Lee. Just as we arrived in view of the sign, I ripped off the blindfold, and in perfect synchronicity, Peggy Lee was singing, "Is that all there is to a circus?" Now I'm sure if I was a guy, Pleasant would have proposed to me right then and there. The neighborhood is a little dodgy but worth the risk.

IKEA (600 N. San Fernando Blvd., Burbank, 818-842-4532, www.ikea.com) Doesn't Ikea mean " fancy milk crates" in Swedish? Upwardly mobile furniture for miles! Now, here's a place that should have rest stops.

BARNES & NOBLE (Media City Center, 731 N. San Fernando Blvd., 818-558-1383, www.barnesandnoble.com) Great place for coffee and reading books you'll never buy in large comfy chairs, which by the way are always taken. I'm convinced that there's a small family living in the chairs in the front window lobby area.

RAGTIME COWBOY (5213 Lankershim Blvd., N. Hollywood, 818-769-6552) Joe (the owner) has been dubbed the

Fashion Guru of NoHo. But he's so much more than that! Whatever you need, Joe has it. Great vintage clothing mixed with hats, shoes, antique quilts, and bedspreads, glamour and clown wigs, clown suits, Frankenstein shoes and costumes that you didn't even know existed but that you must have immediately. The prices are amazing and Joe immediately makes you feel like you've known him all your life!

HISTORIC AND CULT POINTS OF INTEREST

SPAHN RANCH Where the Manson Family lived and fled to during the Tate-LaBianca murders in 1969. Located along the south side of Santa Susanna Pass Road near the entrance to **Iverson Movie Ranch**, the movie/tourist sets burned down in the wildfires of 1970. Since that time, the property has been subdivided into at least three separate parcels. I once went there with writer Legs McNeil and skinhead rednecks chased us out. Kind of fitting.

TOPANGA CANYON The anti-establishment, hippie settling ground. Known for pagan rituals, VW buses with tie-dyed flags, witches, love-ins, Indians, members of the Manson Family, UFO and Jim Morrison sightings. In the '20s Hollywood stars were known to have hideaway cabins for secret affairs, some of which are probably still standing. During War II, mobster Mickey Cohen owned and operated a casino and brothel there. In the '50s, artists and intellectuals lived there waiting out the McCarthy era. In the '70s, Topanga Canyon became the home for the likes of Neil Young, Gram Parsons, the Eagles, and Linda Ronstadt. It's still a beautiful, curve-filled ride from the Valley to the Ocean.

LAKE VIEW TERRACE Put on the map as a result of being the site of the famous Rodney King beating, which led to the LA Riots in '92.

405 FREEWAY OJ Simpson took that historic drive in

the white Bronco down the 405 freeway with a gun held to his head pleading his innocence in the Nicole Brown Simpson and Ron Goldman murders. And just so ya know - avoid at all costs during rush hour - it turns into a parking lot!

RESEDA A nowhere spot on the road, until the January 17, 1994 earthquake shook it into the headlines… was also used as the backdrop for the setting of the film *Boogie Nights*.

BURBANK, HOME OF THE MOB In 1952, the California crime commission singled out Burbank as being a hangout for the Mafia.

TOLUCA LAKE In 1932, Amelia Earhart, the Valley's pre-eminent aviation celebrity, was the first woman to fly the Atlantic solo. In an attempt to fly around the globe, she vanished. At the time of her disappearance she lived with her husband in Toluca Lake, at 10042 Spring Valley Lane.

PACOIMA Singer Ritchie Valens was born and raised in Pacoima. On February 3, 1959 at the age of 17, he was killed in a historic plane crash along with Rock'n'Roll legends Buddy Holly and the Big Bopper.

NORTH HOLLYWOOD Now called the NoHo Arts District, it used to be known as "The Porn Capital of the World."

CANOGA PARK The Porn Capital of the World.

THE BLACK DAHLIA DRANK HERE
Iris Berry

Being a native Los Angeles girl, I've always been fasci-
nated with old Hollywood and old LA. Sometimes I think I'm
in love with a city that doesn't exist anymore. I miss the historical monuments and places that should have (but didn't) make
it and are now gone forever. Some of my favorite places have
been laid to rest, but fortunately many haven't.

Schwab's Drugstore (8024 Sunset Blvd., Hollywood)
once stood where the Virgin Megastore is now. Legend has it
that Lana Turner was discovered here, but it isn't true, that was
just a great publicity story that refuses to die. I spent many of
my teenage days here stealing make-up and sipping coffee at
the counter with a wild assortment of Vaudevillian has-beens,
many of them promising to make me a star!

TO LOS ANGELES

The Garden of Allah (8150-52 Sunset Blvd., Hollywood) was a 25-bungalow party house to the stars, and the party lasted 32 years (1927-1959) with such residents as Marlene Dietrich, Humphrey Bogart, Lauren Bacall, the Marx Brothers, Greta Garbo and F. Scott Fitzgerald. It now exists only as a miniature in a glass case, housed in the bank building where the Garden once stood. I'm sure that I lived there in a past life (and I'm still hungover from it).

Formosa Café (7156 Santa Monica Blvd., West Hollywood, 323-850-9050) Open since 1939, and featured prominently in the movie *LA Confidential*. A Hollywood version of a Chinese restaurant/bar, Philip Marlow style. Rumor has it that Elvis once tipped one of the waitresses a Cadillac, not bad for a day's pay. My favorite place for good Chinese food and sick, kitschy celebrity memorabilia.

Farmers Market (300 N. Fairfax Ave., LA) LA's oldest outdoor market was built in 1934, and is still one of the more popular tourist destinations. Recently remodeled with an all-new outdoor mall connected to the famous landmark, called "The Grove." Complete with movie theatres, fountains with dancing waters, FAO Schwarz, Nordstroms and so much more… a little new world with your old world. Farmers Market has Hollywood souvenirs in every shape and form, for all your Hollywood Sign needs. One of my favorite places to eat and buy stuff likes key chains, salt and pepper shakers, fresh fruit, and toffee.

Bullocks Wilshire (3050 Wilshire Blvd., Miracle Mile/Mid City) Art Deco masterpiece built in 1929. The first "suburban" department store in the United States. It managed to stay open through the culturally devoid 1980s, complete with valet parking and Chandleresque elevator men. No longer open for business, it still stands looking quite regal for your visual pleasure. I have fond memories of eating lunch with my mother in their exquisite "Tea Room" on the top floor, occasionally being interrupted at the table by a fashion model displaying the latest in Chanel, with a view of the city all around.

Magic Castle (7001 Franklin Ave., Hollywood, www.magiccastle.com, 323-851-3313) A private club for magicians and those who appreciate magic. Built in 1909, it resembles a Victorian haunted mansion and houses a restaurant, three theaters, a museum, and library. They also give magic classes and seminars. My goal is to one day be sawed in half here…

2nd Street Tunnel (located underneath Bunker Hill, Downtown LA) One city block long. Many a famous car chase has been filmed through this tunnel. It was my first tunnel experience as a small child. My goal is to one day be chased through here.

Paramount Studios (5555 Melrose Ave., Hollywood, 323-956-5575) it's the last big name studio that's still actually located in Hollywood. One of my first jobs was here… although somehow I managed to never do my work and never get caught. I would lock my office door and climb out of my window to do things like hang out with the cast of *Happy Days* watching them play basketball with Nick Nolte while drinking champagne with the Fonz. That was a great job. My goal is to one day get rehired here.

Hollywood Roosevelt Hotel (7000 Hollywood Blvd., Hollywood, 323-466-7000) Located right on the Walk of Fame, across from Graumann's Chinese Theatre. For the true Hollywood experience, book yourself a room in this twelve-story, Spanish-style hotel built in 1927. The Clark Gable/Carol Lombard suite is only $1500 a night… yeah right! My goal is to either afford to stay here one day, or haunt here, whichever comes first.

Musso & Frank's Grill (6667 Hollywood Blvd., Hollywood, 323-467-5123) Oldest restaurant in Hollywood, since 1919. In the '30s and '40s, it was a famous hangout for writers like William Faulkner, F. Scott Fitzgerald, and Budd Schulberg. To this day, it has the finest reputation for its food and atmosphere. As the saying goes, "After God made the world, he rested at Musso's." Dining here on my 25th birthday, Pleasant had me paged over the intercom. When I picked up the phone, she whispered, "So, do you feel important?" Definitely a good place to get paged.

Angel's Flight (Northwest corner of Third and Hill Sts, Downtown) this is one of the rare examples where LA has rebuilt a landmark it tore down. The two-car railway goes from Hill Street up to Bunker Hill. At only 25 cents, it's the cheapest ride in town, and the view from the top is my favorite LA view.

Echo Park (1100 block Echo Park Ave., Echo Park) Like most city parks that have their own lake, this one provides a romantic paddleboat ride with a front row picturesque view of the Downtown Los Angeles skyline. My favorite first date took place here.

Phillipe The Original (1001 N. Alameda St., Downtown, 323-628-3781) Original home of the French Dip Sandwich, in business since 1908. A cup of coffee is still only ten cents (take that, Starbucks!) My favorite place for a good lamb dip sandwich and old circus photos.

Hollywood Forever Memorial Park (6000 Santa Monica Blvd., Hollywood, 323-469-1181) Formerly known as Hollywood Cemetery, this is the final resting place for folks like Bugsy Siegel, Rudolph Valentino, Tyrone Power, Virginia Rappe, Douglas Fairbanks, Peter Lorre, and many other stars, as well as a number of Armenian Mafia dons. One of my least favorite first dates took place here.

Hollywood Bowl (2301 Hollywood Blvd., Hollywood, www.Hollywoodbowl.com, 323-850-2000) Famous for its musical events of many different varieties. From rock to jazz and classical to the yearly Mariachi Festival. I saw Donovan here with my mom when I was 10 years old and got my first contact high from all the pot smoke.

Baroque Books (1643 Las Palmas Blvd., Hollywood))nce a great book store for all the classics. Owned by beat legend Red Stodolsky. I bought my first Bukowski book here and at one time it was the only place where you could get his books. The store closed down years ago, when Red passed away leaving a huge hole in the city, but his spirit still lives on.

The Frolic Room (6245 Hollywood Blvd., Hollywood, 323-462-5890) You can't miss this place, it's got some of the best neon in town, and has been featured in a number of films. A little closet of a bar right smack dab next to the Pantages Theatre, known for its Hirshfeld wallpaper with caricatures of Jayne Mansfield, Frank Sinatra, the Marx Brothers, and Laurel and Hardy to name a few, whooping it up. If you're looking for old Hollywood, the Frolic Room is one of the last holdouts. This is one of my favorite places to read bathroom graffiti.

Miceli's Restaurant (1646 Las Palmas Blvd., Hollywood, 323-466-3438) One of the older Hollywood restaurants still around. Great Italian food and great atmosphere. I love to eat dinner here at twilight with the view of the Las Palmas bookstand through the stained glass windows. It's like stepping back in time.

Bob's Big Boy (4211 Riverside Drive, Toluca Lake, 818-843-9334) With its running tradition since 1958, every Friday night is Cruise Night. The parking lot is crawling with custom cars and hot rods. After my high school reunion ended in a brawl that I was responsible for (the police had to come and break it up), we all came here to eat and talk about how much fun we had. Now that's a memory I'll always cherish.

Cinerama Dome Theatre (6360 Sunset Blvd., Hollywood, 323-464-4226) The world's first Cinerama theater with a unique shape, a huge white dome looking a lot like half a giant golf ball. Recently remodeled and now attached to a brand new modern mall. Pity - but at least it wasn't torn down, as was the original plan! My mother took my babysitter and me her to see *Easy Rider* when it first came out.

MALEN FUCKENSHEMALE
Vaginal Davis

I knew it was going to happen. My little neighborhood of Guadalamara Canal is officially gentrified. [*Writers Note to Editor: I'm *not* the only one who calls this part of town Guadalamara, I couldn't make that up if I tried.] My Eastside neighborhood is bordered by Silverlake's Virgil Village on the East, Hancock Park on the West, Koreatown to the South, and Hollywood to the North you could easily get caught between warring Mexican and El Salvadoran street gangs who are fighting over drug turf abandoned by the corrupt police of the infamous Rampart scandal. Wide streets are lined with statuesque palm trees, where entire families of voluptuous rats make their nests. Isn't it beautiful?

Unfortunately, it will never be the same again. I've only

myself to blame, for writing about my little neck of the woods. Oh, and Mrs. *LA Times*, who recently did a profile on how this smarmy little carpetbagger from the Bay Area is buying up old apartment buildings in my area, and renovating them so he can charge high Westside rents. Goodbye Latin American immigrants, hello organic food stores. What really irks me is when I see some cute muscular piece of high snow, new in my 'hood, and he's immediately all friendly and Chatty Cathy with me until he figures out I'm not a black drug dealer but just a desperate homo on the prowl for dorky white dick… and then he turns sour, distant and aloof.

So this time around, I'm going to profile a few of the people who live and work in my part of town. I'll also include some places off the beaten path that you may or may not have noticed or wondered about, but that you dismissed.

If you decide to move from Mar Vista to Normandie and Third, do so at your own peril, because if you are not willing to have sex with me and I find you attractive I may be forced to kill you. My bohemian 'hood is a historic part of town that was once a working class Irish section of the city. Now it's populated by recent Latin American and Eastern European immigrants, East Indians, Vietnamese, and Filipinos. Some of the city's most amazing denizens reside in or near this area of town. They are the kind of people who take the old cliché of LA as a dream factory and turn it inside out, only their dreamscapes are more phantasmagoric. Since I'm the only native Angeleno who has never owned or driven a car, I love nothing more than riding on my vintage bicycle up and down my area surveying its tatty splendour.

I usually start my ride off on Beverly Boulevard, stopping by the **Einar C. Petersen Studio Court** (4350 Beverly Blvd., LA). The complex was built in 1922 in the Hansel and Gretel Style and is on the county register as a historical landmark.

Only visual artists live or work in the compound and is the current home to the **Chicken Boy Store and Pug Emporium**, a collective run by and for artists and their admirers. Then there are the studios of Gary and David Leonard. The Leonards are a father and son photography tag team. Gary was one of the first LA photographers to capture the city's seminal punk scene in the late '70s. His continuing photo series, "Take My Picture" appearing in the alternative weekly paper the *New Times,* can be both lurid and whimsical. His 21-year-old son David is following in his father's footsteps generally making a pest of himself around the town. Not that anyone minds: he is a gorgeous young blond boy with an amazing body and cruel club endowment that he's not afraid to showcase. Whenever you see him out he wears very little clothing and that gets even more attention than the subjects he photographs. In fact, to get into the prestigious art school California Institute of the Arts, he mailed himself butt naked to the admissions office in a giant wooden crate.

If you were in a car you would never notice the lovely **Petersen Studio Courtyard** with its cottages built to give the appearance of a rustic Bavarian Village. Since the artifice of the movie industry hovers over the entire city like an inversion layer of grime, a lot of buildings in LA like the Petersen look like they are cast-offs from a movie set. It's just that quality that attracted painter/actress Mary Woronov and performance artist Johanna Went, who have had their studios here for twenty years. Woronov is best known for her appearances in Andy Warhol's *Chelsea Girls*, and starring with the Ramones in *Rock-n-Roll High School*. Went electrified audiences since the early 1980s when she would open for punk bands with her shamanistic comic rituals which use huge props, masses of trash, and buckets of fake blood.

Across the street and a few blocks down is the **Beverly**

TO LOS ANGELES

Hot Springs (308 North Oxford, 323-734-7000, www.beverlyhotsprings.com), which sits on top of a natural alkaline mineral hot spring. It's rumored that top celebrities like John Travolta, George Michael, Danny Masterson from *That 70s Show*, Giovanni Ribisi and Tom Cruise have been caught in compromising positions in the men's locker room.

New to the Guadalamara area is the sexy young academe, Professor Jennifer Doyle, who teaches American literature at UC Riverside. Professor Doyle loves to act as a prettier version of Gertrude Stein, holding court salon-style and hosting many international scholars, intellectuals and bon vivants at her home for gourmet feasts. You never know who will be at her house for dinner. This last visit she had her Flemish cousin Mathilde d'Udekem d'Acoz, formal title: The Duchess of Brabant. She is the wife of Crown Prince Phillippe of Belgium, and is a sweet and unassuming young lady in the style of the late Lady Diana Spencer. What makes Jennifer a sexy new style academic? Well, first of all, she is always talking about sex and that's sexy. In the classroom she encourages her students to develop "a voice for representing pleasure and desire." I've been invited to her school many times as a visiting artist and I don't know how she manages to keep her professional composure surrounded by so many young hot humpy boys. Professor Doyle incorporates contemporary art into teaching American literature. Her department hired her especially because of her wacky underground background in performance art and art history. She's written extensively on Andy Warhol, editing a book of essays called *Pop-Out: Queer Warhol*. She's currently writing a book called Sex *Objects: Aesthetics and the Problem of Interest*. It's basically a book about having bad sex. Naomi Schor calls it "Clit Crit." So if you are finding it too dry at Harvard or Yale, and want to study with a professor who classifies herself as part Marxist, part feminist, part Foucoultian and queer in her intellectual orientation then you need to hook up with Jennifer Doyle.

Though she doesn't live in my neighborhood, but in the east side area known as Frogtown, (Atwater Village), Bibbe Hansen is the most important woman in Los Angeles. She comes from Bohemian royalty. Her mother Audrey Hansen, half-Swedish, half-Jewish, was the famed Thumbelina dancer on the old Perry Como TV show in the early 1950s. In the 1940s, Bibbe's mother used to do an act with two gay brothers Donald and Harold where they would all dress up as sailors and do this very Jean Genet-ish routine that was a mixture of Querelle and Last Exit to Brooklyn - It was way ahead of its time. Her father was the Fluxus pioneer Al Hansen. As a New York pre-teen and teenager in the '60s, she was the youngest of Andy Warhol's superstars leading a juvenile life of crime and debauchery that included a recording contract to Columbia's Colpix label with the all-girl group The Whippets along with Janet Kerouac. They had a hit single called "I Wanna Talk With You" which was the answer to the Beatles "I Wanna Hold Your Hand". She also did Happenings with her father and experimental theatre at Judson Church, LaMama, and Living Theatre in New York. Her Warhol films included *10 Beautiful Girls* and *10 More Beautiful Girls*, Andy Warhol's *L'Aventura* which takes place at the L'Aventura Restaurant on 2nd Avenue and D of course, and *Andy Warhol's Prison* with Edie Sedgewick. She eventually settled down to marriage and children in LA in the early '70s, but left her husband, pop star Beck's father David Campbell, for a 15-year-old Chicano boy named Sean Carrillo who she is now married to. Bibbe and Sean ran a restaurant and performance art/rock venue called Troy Cafe in Little Tokyo for eight years, which was the only cool thing in LA at the time. I've known Bibbe since the late 1970s when she was den mother to punk bands The Germs and The Screamers. She even formed her own art punk band,

Black Fag, in the early '90s as a gag on her junior pop star son Beck. She's just finished traveling the world with the art show *Playing With Matches*. Besides her underground film oeuvre she has appeared in a few Hollywood movies like *Phantom of the Paradise* directed by Brian De Palma who she says, "gives good head."

AREA UPDATES AND DISCLOSURES

Eco-Village Demonstration (Whitehouse Place and Bimini St.) Lois Arkin's intentional sustainable community-in-process received national attention a few years ago because of their battling with the LA Unified School District, who wanted them to vacate the premises so they could add to Virgil Middle School, directly across the street. Well, Lois & Company won the first round of battles, and lately have been keeping a low profile. I think Ms. Arkin is running a white slavery ring. I see a lot of humpy skater boys hanging around her fourplex.

The Love Boat Building (3919 West 8th St.) This streamlined '20s Moderne nautical apartment building is home to famous conceptual artist Larry Johnson. He heads the Photo Department of Otis Parsons and is The Love Boat's resident manager. The other famous tenant is filmmaker/DJ/club promoter Jeffreyland Hilbert UK.

Chapman Market (between Kenmore and Alexandria Street on 6th St.) The oldest mini-mall in Los Angeles, built in the 1920s. The Market houses trendy Korean stores, nightclubs, and restaurants, and is a hotspot for suburban Korean youth. Across the street at the Chapman Studios is the clothing store Man Trap, which sells hissy knockoffs of fashion-forward Euro designers. There is also photography gallery and print shop, and in the Bell Tower is the live-in photo studio of photographer Raul Vega, who has been there since the early '70s. Before I knew Raul I remember walking by his studio one day after

Junior High in 1975 and seeing the pop/soul group The Silvers and their management team scurrying up his stairs.

Taylor's Steakhouse (3361 West 8th St., 323-382-8449, www.taylorssteakhouse.com) Old school steakhouse in the Raymond Chandler vein. There was a memorable Korean Mafia shootout in the place in the early 1980s. My two favorite waitresses are the middle-aged tranny who *almost* passes, and Josh of Danzig's mother.

The Escape Room (4083 West 3rd St. - bottom of Rudyard Kipling Residence Hotel, 213-386-1594) has a small dance floor, karaoke and strong SSI drinks.

Frank & Hank (523 South Western, 213-383-2087) Charles Bukowski bar with unflattering fluorescent lighting. (Editor's note: one of the few bars in LA where smoking is not only allowed but encouraged.)

The Monte Carlo II (3450 West Sixth St., 213-389-4553) Owned by two Malaysian girls who can never get your drink order right and who never wash their cocktail glasses. Watch out for the muscular ultra-friendly Greek guy, he's a nefarious pickpocket — oh, and if a portly black lady wants to share her pipe: beware — it's got crack cocaine in it. An actress with the East Berlin Ensemble thought she was smoking hash and had to be rushed to the emergency room.

GUADALAMARA REHAB UPDATES

Recovery Row's Friendly House (439 South Normandie, 213-389-9964) 90-day recovery house for women only. Courtney Love and a lot of other Hollywood punk girls have spent quality time here.

Portals (269 South Mariposa, 213-381-8400) as well as **Portals Club House** are housed in two Craftsmen mansions built in the teens. The Double Trudgers Unit is still going strong.

Christian Crisis (145 South Kenmore) You must either

be Born Again or have a pinhead to receive treatment here.

Delancey Street Foundation (400 North Vermont, 323-662-4888) Sexiest rehab only for the hunkiest, beefiest, most well-endowed felons trying to restore their societal privileges in an uber-masculine setting. Lush views of the Hollywood Freeway.

RELIGIOUS ORGANIZATIONS

Islamic Center of Southern California (434 South Vermont Ave.) Jean Genet didn't give his support to the Palestinians and Black Panthers because he believed in their causes. He supported them because they occasionally threw him a mercy bone. Allah be praised!

St. George's Bulgarian Eastern Orthodox Church (150 South Alexandria) Uri, the groundskeeper *still* visits me late at night. I don't look a 14-1/2 inch hung gift horse in the mouth.

OFF THE BEATEN SWATH

Melabon Lechon Filipino High-tech Mini Mall (130 South Vermont) I love it when Filipinos speaking Tagalog can't understand each other until they've repeated themselves at least three times.

The Wiltern Theatre (3790 Wilshire Blvd., 213-380-5005) This Art Deco gem narrowly escaped the wrecking ball in the late 1970s. The former movie palace has been reincarnated as a concert venue, but occasionally plays host to M.O.C.A.'s Momma On The Couch plays, which are designed for a predominantly black urban audience. The phrase "mama on the couch" comes from George C. Wolfe's famous play, *The Colored Museum*, which includes a sketch called "The Last Mama On The Couch Play", dealing with black realism and how it's depicted in an inner city theater. These plays are centered on religion, have great music, and are filled with neck-rollin', finger-wavin' comedy. Each includes an all-important message involving a "troubled young man" who has usually gone astray in prodigal son fashion. And they all close with an emotionally rousing speech by his mama. I've become addicted to these tired plays with titles like *Wicked Ways Mama*, *I Want to Sing*, *Is That Man Your Husband?* and *God Don't Like Ugly*.

The Fugly House of Carthay Circle (865 West Hayes Dr., LA) Amidst a beautiful array of 1920s homes is this modern monstrosity. When was it built? Why was it built? I guess every man deserves his castle, but discretion is the better part of valor. I've never seen anyone come in or out of this house, and it seems like it's always in a perpetual state of disrepair.

Asthma Vapineze (1026 North Fairfax, West Hollywood) This is an unassuming bungalow in a mixed residential and commercial section of Fairfax Avenue. I've always wondered what the neon sign was all about. The salty dog owner says it's an asthma treatment center that has been there since 1935. And from the look of the rug on his prune head, it's the same one he's been wearing since 1935. Last time I passed by he had covered up the sign with a tarp. Now, *that's* paranoid.

The Strawberry Shortcake Compound (507 North Rodeo Dr., Beverly Hills) Sitting right off of Santa Monica Blvd., a bitch slap away from the Beverly Hills City Hall and Public Library. Is it Gaudy or gaudy? You be the judge.

The Rose Gardens of Exposition Park (Jefferson Blvd. and Vermont across from USC, South Central LA) Tucked between the Museum of Science and Industry, the Sports Arena and the Coliseum is this veritable oasis of visual splendor, featuring roses of all shapes sizes and colors. A favorite haunt for Latino wedding and quinceniera photos.

About the Authors

E.A. GEHMAN somehow managed to retire from Hollywood before the age of forty without either a tit-job or a lengthy stint in rehab. She doesn't live at the Beverly Hills Hotel anymore, but there have been reports of recent sightings.

KAREN CUSOLITO is a native Angeleno who used to prowl the streets as a crime reporter for the late, great Los Angeles *Herald Examiner*. She now teaches English at the world famous Hollywood High School.

SHAWNA KENNEY is the author of the award-winning *I Was A Teenage Dominatrix* (Last Gasp). Her work has appeared in numerous pop culture magazines and websites.

M.X. LINGUA periodically emerges from the lower fourth dimension to have a cocktail in Los Angeles.

AIDA CYNTHIA DE SANTIS is a crazy cartoonist and singer/songwriter for the art band Kittenfreaky. She *does* live on the West Side.

CLINT CATALYST is a Southern-fried prancy boy with honey in his hips and bile in his tongue. He is the author of *Cottonmouth Kisses* (Manic D Press) and lots of other B.S.

NANCY WHALEN writes fictional short stories and journalistic pieces with the goal of bringing to light the special phenomena in everyday life. **ANTHONY BERNAL** helped her write the vintage and thrift store chapter.

DAVID L. ULIN would rather read than eat. He moved to Los Angeles in 1991.

SUZY BEAL is an artist and writer with a life-long interest in Los Angeles history. She claims dual citizenship of Silverlake and the South Bay.

LIBBY MOLYNEAUX is a writer/editor at *LA Weekly*. Her husband **JOE HILL** advises all cyclists to wear helmets.

They live in Laurel Canyon.

VAGINAL DAVIS is a ghetto provocateuse who destroys the lives of innocent young white boys, leading them into madness or death.

IRIS BERRY is the author of *Two Blocks East Of Vine* (Incommunicado Press) as well as the forthcoming collection of short stories *In The Shadow Of The Hollywood Sign.*

S.A.GRIFFIN is a crash vampire living in LA. He is a father, husband and human being.

BARNES is an LA underground faggot from Toronto with a deep performance and rock'n'roll resume. He is a journalist and leads the bands Loudboy and Blue Radio.

JAYSON MARSTON is always as twisted and kinky as possible. He is a writer, sex worker, activist, and works with A.I.M.

LAURAN HOFFMAN is a writer/per former who falls in love easily, frequently and obsessively. She is the author of the play and movie *Bar Girls* (Orion Classics).

DAN EPSTEIN, record weasel extraordinaire, is a freelance journalist who has written for numerous magazines and newspapers. Terrifyingly enough, he has a huge soft spot in his heart for Nick Guilder.

MARY HERCZOG is a journalist, travel writer, poet and bon vivant who lives in Los Angeles.

PLEASANT GEHMAN is the author of the books *Senorita Sin*, *Princess of Hollywood*, and *Escape From Houdini Mountain*. In addition to freelance writing and co-editing Puppet Terror, she bellydances, paints, sings and loves dirty boys. She lives with four cats and a ventriloquist dummy named Holly Woodhead.

Index

THE UNDERGROUND GUIDE

TO LOS ANGELES

THE UNDERGROUND GUIDE

THE UNDERGROUND GUIDE